SHALL NOT BE DENIED

WOMEN FIGHT FOR THE VOTE

Wage-earning women picketing during a labor themed picket day, February 18, 1917.

SHALL NOT BE DENIED

WOMEN FIGHT FOR THE VOTE

Official Companion to the Library of Congress Exhibition

Foreword by Carla D. Hayden

RUTGERS UNIVERSITY PRESS • LIBRARY OF CONGRESS
NEW BRUNSWICK, CAMDEN, AND NEWARK, NEW JERSEY, AND LONDON

FOR WOMEN
PROCESSION
SQUARE TO CAPITOL
DAY MAY 9
RTS 3 P. M.
CEDED BY
G BELASCO TH
REGISTER
12,30 O'CLOCK P. M.

CONTENTS

Suffragists posting a billboard advertising the May 9, 1914, march at the US Capitol (detail).

FOREWORD

In 1903 the sixth Librarian of Congress, Ainsworth Spofford, convinced his friend, suffrage leader Susan B. Anthony, to donate her personal collection of more than 250 books and other printed material to the Library. As Anthony prepared her donation, she inscribed many of the books with commentary on their history and importance, creating a valuable record of the suffrage leader's reflections on a lifetime of activism.

The Library's curators soon began amassing manuscripts, scrapbooks, photographs, and other items relating to the struggle for women's rights, including the papers of Carrie Chapman Catt, Mary Church Terrell, and other suffragists, as well as the records of the National American Woman Suffrage Association and the National Woman's Party. Together these items form a compelling documentary history of the suffrage movement from its early connections to the abolition and temperance campaigns to the passage of the Nineteenth Amendment—nicknamed the Anthony Amendment—in August 1920.

Women fought for more than seventy years to enshrine their voting rights in the United States, and the movement's earliest crusaders didn't live to enjoy the fruits of their long labors. The history of this

Gordon Grant, *Giddap! Friendly Farmer.—Can't I give ye a lift, girls? Suffragette "General."—You can, sir, by voting for the Cause!* Published in *Puck*, March 15, 1914 (detail).

Martha Wentworth Suffern, vice chairman of the Woman Suffrage Party of New York, demonstrating in 1914.

struggle is one of celebration and setbacks, commanded by dynamic and formidable personalities—change-makers—who believed in relentless action and civil disobedience in the name of equality and justice. In fighting for the right to vote, women formed national political organizations, developed new strategies for protest, and brought women into the public sphere in new and more visible ways. These advances laid the groundwork for civic action that has been emulated by those working for other civil rights causes. I encourage you to visit the Library in person or online at www.loc.gov to learn more about the change-makers who have shaped US history.

Carla D. Hayden
Librarian of Congress

Kenneth Russell Chamberlain, *Revised*, published in *Puck*, April 14, 1917.

Chapter 1

BUILDING A MOVEMENT

Despite the notions of equality that inspired America's war for independence from Great Britain, American women had few, if any, rights. Women had no legal identity separate from their husbands and were unable to sign contracts, own property, access formal education, obtain divorces easily, or win custody of their children after divorce well into the nineteenth century. Several individuals challenged these norms in the country's earliest days, and a cumulative desire to address this inequality and challenge the country to live up to its revolutionary promise eventually led to a two-day convention in Seneca Falls, New York, in 1848, where 300 women and men gathered in support of women's rights. These supporters became increasingly organized during the latter half of the nineteenth century—relying heavily on their experience in both the abolition and temperance movements—and rallied around the cause of votes for women.

Women who lent their support to abolishing slavery also believed universal suffrage would follow, but both the Fourteenth and Fifteenth Amendments ignored their demand for voting rights; in fact, the Fourteenth Amendment injected the word "male" into the Constitution for the first time. Suffrage leaders responded differently, leading to a split in the movement. In 1878, the first federal woman suffrage amendment was introduced in Congress but was soundly defeated. As the nineteenth century neared an end, suffragists reunited under the National American Woman Suffrage Association (NAWSA), and the groundwork was laid for a national movement.

Louis Dalrymple, *A Suggestion to the Buffalo Exposition*, published in *Puck*, April 3, 1901 (detail).

Remember the Ladies

In early America, free women's legal and political standing depended on their marital status. Most married women could not own property, a common requirement for voting; enslaved women, considered property themselves, essentially had no legal rights. Between 1777 and 1807, women lost the right to vote in the few states that had permitted it.

But in an age of revolution, not all women accepted the status quo. Abigail Adams called upon her husband John to "Remember the Ladies" while at the Continental Congress in 1776—he acknowledged her plea, but women were not represented in the nation's founding documents. Two decades later, Abigail Adams declared to her sister in a July 19,

Margaret Brent (ca. 1601–1671) had an unusual position as a landowning single woman in seventeenth-century St. Mary's City, Maryland. Known to represent herself in court, she was appointed Lord Baltimore's attorney, and in 1648 requested two votes in the Maryland assembly—one for herself, and one for her client. The governor declined and Brent eventually settled in Virginia, near Brent Point, seen on the left side of this detail of Emanuel Bowen's *New and Accurate Map of Virginia & Maryland* (1752).

1799 letter, "I will never consent to have our sex considered in an inferiour point of light. Let each planet shine in their own orbit. God and nature designd it so—If man is Lord, woman is *Lordess*." Like Adams, a few women questioned the limits of law and tradition.

British philosopher Mary Wollstonecraft (1759–1797; left, stipple engraving by William Ridley, 1796) wrote *A Vindication of the Rights of Woman: With Strictures on Political and Moral Subjects* (1792) to advocate for women's education and their equal standing with men. Her treatise was an inspiration to early suffragists, especially Susan B. Anthony, who hung Wollstonecraft's picture in her home and noted in her copy of *A Vindication* (right) that she was "a great admirer of this earliest work for woman's right to Equality of rights."

The 1787 US Constitutional Convention granted states the power to define voting rights. At that time, New Jersey was the only state that allowed voting by all inhabitants meeting certain age, property, and residency requirements. When the *Acts of the Council and General Assembly of the State of New-Jersey* (right) was published in 1784, select New Jersey women could vote. This ended in 1807 when a state law restricted the vote to "free, white, male citizens" at least 21 years old and "worth fifty pounds."

Enslaved woman Elizabeth Freeman (ca. 1742–1829; portrait at left by Susan Anne Livingston Ridley Sedgwick, 1811), known as "Mum Bett," enlisted the help of attorney Thomas Sedgwick to petition for her freedom under the Massachusetts Constitution, which declared that "all men are born free and equal." In 1781, Freeman won her suit, freeing her from bondage to Colonel John Ashley and setting a precedent against the legal defense of slavery in the Commonwealth of Massachusetts.

Am I Not a Woman and a Sister?

The fight to abolish slavery provided women with opportunities to step outside the domestic sphere and to consider the parallels between the oppression of women and of the enslaved. Though their roles were contested, women were instrumental to the abolitionist movement. Free African American and Quaker communities had long worked to end slavery before radical activists brought new urgency to the cause in the 1830s by calling for immediate emancipation. Individuals such as Lucretia Mott founded local female auxiliaries of the American Anti-Slavery Society—only five years after its founding in 1833, more than one hundred auxiliaries had been established.

Some women, including Maria W. Stewart and Sarah and Angelina Grimké, spoke publicly in favor of abolition, challenging traditional gender norms. In *Religion and the Pure*

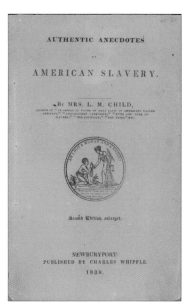

AUTHENTIC ANECDOTES

AMERICAN SLAVERY.

By MRS. L. M. CHILD,

NEWBURYPORT:
PUBLISHED BY CHARLES WHIPPLE
1838.

Lydia Maria Child (1802–1880), a popular novelist and author of household advice books, championed the abolitionist cause with influential texts, including *An Appeal in Favor of That Class of Americans Called Africans* (1833) and *Authentic Anecdotes of American Slavery* (1838, left). Child also wrote a comparative history of women, full of examples of oppression and achievement, in 1835. Like Mott, Child believed that women should be equal partners in the fight to end slavery.

Principles of Morality (1831), Stewart called for fellow black women to unite to end slavery: "Ye daughters of Africa, awake! Awake! Arise! No longer sleep nor slumber, but distinguish yourself. Show forth to the world that ye are endowed with noble and exalted faculties."

Lucretia Mott.

"Has the slave been oppressed so long that he cannot appreciate the blessings of Liberty? And has woman been so long crushed, enervated, paralyzed, prostrated by the influences by which she has been surrounded, that she too is ready to say she would not have any more rights if she could?"

—Lucretia Mott, "The Laws in Relation to Women," delivered at the National Woman's Rights Convention, Cleveland, Ohio, 1853

Quaker minister Lucretia Mott (1793–1880; pictured ca. 1875) was a founding member of the Philadelphia Female Anti-Slavery Society (1833), which resolved "that the Anti-Slavery enterprise presents one of the most appropriate fields for the exertion of the influence of woman." In 1840, Mott met Elizabeth Cady Stanton when both attended the World's Anti-Slavery Convention in London, where Mott and other women delegates were refused seats. Mott drew comparisons between the discrimination faced by enslaved African Americans and by women in her powerful speeches and writing.

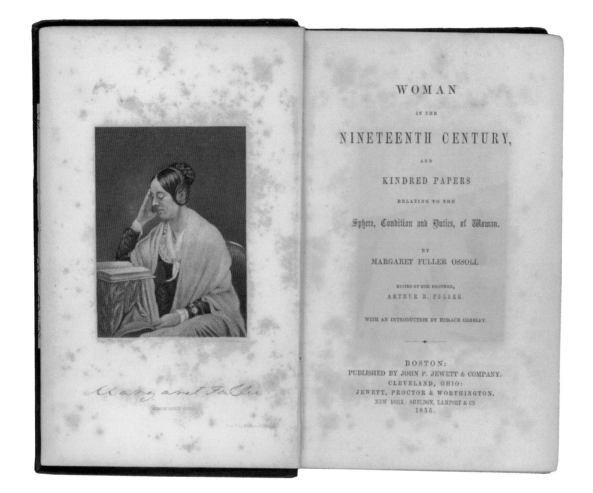

Critic Margaret Fuller (1810–1850) articulated her theory for women's equality in *Woman in the Nineteenth Century* (1845), where she declared, "We would have every arbitrary barrier thrown down. We would have every path laid open to woman as freely as to man." A Transcendentalist, Fuller was inspired by the radical rethinking of social norms within the abolitionist movement, writing, "of all its banners, none has been more steadily upheld, and under none have more valor and willingness for real sacrifices been shown, than that of the champions of the enslaved African. And this band it is, which, partly from a natural following out of principles, partly because many women have been prominent in that cause, makes, just now, the warmest appeal in behalf of Woman."

Seneca Falls

Elizabeth Cady Stanton and her daughter, Harriot. from a daguerreotype 1856.

In advocating for suffrage as a central point in her manifesto, the "Declaration of Sentiments," Elizabeth Cady Stanton (1815–1902) forged ahead of other advocates for women's rights. As the suffragists gathered adherents to the cause, Stanton refused to limit her demands solely to the vote, arguing vigorously for a woman's right to higher education, to a professional life, and to a legal identity that included the right to own property and to obtain divorce. Her daughter Harriot Stanton Blatch, pictured here with her mother in 1856, followed in her mother's footsteps to fight for women's rights.

Many women and men working in the anti-slavery movement eventually became a part of the struggle for equal rights for women. It was five abolitionists—Elizabeth Cady Stanton, Lucretia Mott, her sister Martha C. Wright, and Mott's fellow Quakers Jane Hunt and Mary McClintock—who decided to hold the first women's rights convention, in Seneca Falls, New York. In early July 1848, they wrote a notice in the *Seneca County Courier* advertising a meeting to discuss "the social, civil, and religious condition and rights of women." Despite the minimal publicity, an estimated 300 people attended the two-day convention, considered by many to be the beginning of the American suffrage movement.

The Seneca Falls Convention inspired similar meetings around the country, enabling the movement to grow. The first national women's rights meeting, organized by abolitionists Paulina Wright Davis and Lucy Stone, was held in 1850 in Worcester, Massachusetts. More than 1,000 suffrage supporters from throughout the Northeast, Midwest, and California attended.

6

results necessarily from the fact of the identity of the race in capabilities and responsibilities.

Resolved, therefore, That, being invested by the Creator with the same capabilities, and the same consciousness of responsibility for their exercise, it is demonstrably the right and duty of woman, equally with man, to promote every righteous cause, by every righteous means; and especially in regard to the great subjects of morals and religion, it is self-evidently her right to participate with her brother in teaching them, both in private and in public, by writing and by speaking, by any instrumentalities proper to be used, and in any assemblies proper to be held; and this being a self-evident truth, growing out of the divinely implanted principles of human nature, any custom or authority adverse to it, whether modern or wearing the hoary sanction of antiquity, is to be regarded as self-evident falsehood, and at war with the interests of mankind.

LUCRETIA MOTT read a humorous article from a newspaper, written by MARTHA C. WRIGHT. After an address by E. W. M'CLINTOCK, the meeting adjourned to 10 o'clock the next morning.

In the evening, LUCRETIA MOTT spoke with her usual eloquence and power to a large and intelligent audience on the subject of Reforms in general.

THURSDAY MORNING.

The Convention assembled at the hour appointed, JAMES MOTT, of Philadelphia, in the Chair. The minutes of the previous day having been read, E. C. STANTON again read the Declaration of Sentiments, which was freely discussed by LUCRETIA MOTT, ANSEL BASCOM, S. E. WOODWORTH, THOMAS and MARY ANN M'CLINTOCK,

7

FREDERICK DOUGLASS, AMY POST, CATHARINE STEBBINS, and ELIZABETH C. STANTON, and was unanimously adopted, as follows:

DECLARATION OF SENTIMENTS.

When, in the course of human events, it becomes necessary for one portion of the family of man to assume among the people of the earth a position different from that which they have hitherto occupied, but one to which the laws of nature and of nature's God entitle them, a decent respect to the opinions of mankind requires that they should declare the causes that impel them to such a course.

We hold these truths to be self-evident: that all men and women are created equal; that they are endowed by their Creator with certain inalienable rights; that among these are life, liberty, and the pursuit of happiness; that to secure these rights governments are instituted, deriving their just powers from the consent of the governed.—Whenever any form of Government becomes destructive of these ends, it is the right of those who suffer from it to refuse allegiance to it, and to insist upon the institution of a new government, laying its foundation on such principles, and organizing its powers in such form as to them shall seem most likely to effect their safety and happiness. Prudence, indeed, will dictate that governments long established should not be changed for light and transient causes; and accordingly, all experience hath shown that mankind are more disposed to suffer, while evils are sufferable, than to right themselves by abolishing the forms to which they are accustomed. But when a long train of abuses and usurpations, pursuing invariably the same object, evinces a design to reduce them under absolute despotism, it is their duty to throw off such government, and to provide new guards for their future security. Such has been

Over the course of the two-day convention in Seneca Falls, Stanton's "Declaration of Sentiments" was read and adopted. Modeled after the Declaration of Independence, it protested women's inferior legal status and put forward a list of eleven proposals for the moral, economic, and political equality of women, the most radical of which demanded "the elective franchise." Stanton's original Declaration is believed lost, but this rare printed version, from the *Report of the Woman's Rights Convention, Held at Seneca Falls, New York, July 19 and 20, 1848*, has survived. This copy was printed at the offices of the *North Star*, an abolitionist newspaper founded in 1847 by Frederick Douglass.

Frederick Douglass (ca. 1817–1895; pictured 1862) escaped from slavery in Maryland and settled in Rochester, New York, where he became a leader of the abolitionist movement and an important ally to the women's cause. Douglass attended the meeting at Seneca Falls and spoke forcefully in support of Stanton's most radical resolution, the demand that women have the right to vote—the only resolution that did not pass unanimously.

"Woman alone can understand the height and the depth, the length and the breadth of her own degradation and woe. Man cannot speak for us—because he has been educated to believe that we differ from him so materially, that he cannot judge of our thoughts, feelings and opinions by his own."

—Elizabeth Cady Stanton, speaking in September 1848

Yᴇ MAY SESSION OF Yᴇ WOMAN'S RIGHTS CONVENTION—Yᴇ ORATOR OF Yᴇ DAY DENOUNCING Yᴇ LORDS OF CREATION.

After Seneca Falls, women's rights conventions became annual events, where women met to discuss educational opportunities, divorce reform, property rights, and sometimes labor issues. The conventions that were held throughout the North and West often received unsympathetic reports in the press and encountered disruptive groups in the lecture hall. On June 11, 1859, *Harper's Weekly* published this wood engraving mocking the meetings, with men in both galleries heckling and interrupting the woman at the dais.

Dress Reform and the Bloomer Costume

The daughter of an ardent abolitionist, Elizabeth Smith Miller (1822–1911) grew up in a politically charged household and was a lifelong advocate for and financial supporter of women's rights. She is pictured here in 1851 in a costume of her own design, which she described in the June 1892 issue of *The Arena* as "a dark brown corded silk, short skirt and straight trousers, a short but graceful and richly trimmed French cloak of black velvet with drooping sleeves."

As a mother of young children and an avid gardener, suffragist Elizabeth Smith Miller began wearing a short skirt over loose trousers in the early 1850s. Her cousin Elizabeth Cady Stanton and Stanton's neighbor Amelia Bloomer promptly copied Miller's design. When Bloomer promoted the style as a healthier and more liberated dress alternative to tight corsets and heavy petticoats in her newspaper, *The Lily*, the look became known as the "bloomer costume." Bloomer received hundreds of letters from women asking for sewing patterns, and the paper's circulation increased by thousands. Stanton was wearing bloomers in May 1851 when Bloomer introduced her to her houseguest Susan B. Anthony, beginning the fifty-year Stanton-Anthony partnership in the suffrage campaign.

Eventually, most suffragists returned to wearing long skirts. As Bloomer later wrote in the *Chicago Daily Tribune* (December 8, 1889), "We all felt that the dress was drawing attention from what we thought of far greater importance—the question of woman's right to better education, to a wider field of employment, to better remuneration for her labor, and to the ballot for the protection of her rights."

Even after most prominent suffragists stopped wearing the bloomer costume, some dedicated women continued pressing for dress reform. *Frank Leslie's Illustrated Newspaper* depicted a ladies' dress reform meeting at Freeman Place Chapel in Boston in its June 20, 1874, issue (left). Despite their efforts, dress reform did not gain much traction until the bicycling craze of the 1890s.

Although the bloomer fad was short-lived, it permeated popular culture while it lasted, appearing regularly in newspaper articles and cartoons, both favorable and satirical. Shown here is the cover of the sheet music for the "Bloomer Waltz" (1851, right), composed by William Dessier. At least twenty-five songs were published about the bloomer costume between 1851 and 1853.

Love and Protest in a Suffrage Marriage

A skilled public speaker, Massachusetts-born Lucy Stone was raised in an abolitionist household, and she lectured on both that cause and in support of women's rights. Despite her reluctance to marry due to the oppressive control that marriage laws gave the husband over his wife, she was courted persistently by Henry Blackwell, an abolitionist merchant, and in 1855 she married him. According to their daughter Alice, Blackwell promised Stone that if they married he would help her fight for women's rights, and he had the idea for the couple to fashion an original marriage agreement that gave Stone control of her own property. After consulting with lawyers, Stone kept her maiden name. In this she became a model for others; women who kept their own names were henceforth called "Lucy Stoners."

Henry Browne Blackwell (1825–1909; right) heard Lucy Stone (1818–1893; left) speak at the convention to amend Massachusetts's constitution and asked fellow abolitionist William Lloyd Garrison for a letter of introduction. After a two-year courtship, Stone agreed to marry him. Their marriage suffered from separations, Henry's business failings, and his rumored infidelity. Their only surviving child, Alice Stone Blackwell, followed in the family business of fighting for votes for women.

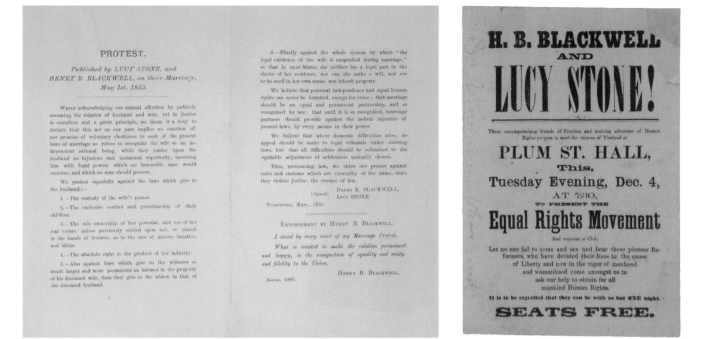

This statement (left)—radical for its time—was read out loud at their May 1, 1855, wedding ceremony in Massachusetts and published widely in newspapers across the country. The couple eliminated the bridal vow "to obey" and circulated a written protest on which both had labored. Similar marriage protests had occurred before, with the weddings of Theodore and Angela Grimké Weld in 1838 and John Stuart and Harriet Mill in 1851. In 1840, Elizabeth Cady Stanton refused to use the word "obey" in her wedding ceremony with anti-slavery activist Henry Stanton.

Stone and Blackwell continued working for abolition and women's rights throughout their long marriage. In 1870, the couple began publishing the *Woman's Journal,* an influential weekly newspaper focusing on suffrage and women's rights, which their daughter Alice Stone Blackwell would later edit. Notably, Lucy Stone's name is larger than her husband's in this announcement for a dual speech "To Present the Equal Rights Movement" at a hall in New Jersey (right)—reflective of her position as the better-known, better-paid lecturer of the pair.

The Movement Splinters

After the Civil War and the emancipation of slaves, supporters of abolition and women's rights created the American Equal Rights Association (AERA) to push for universal suffrage. In its four-year existence, the AERA stirred division and controversy, as members vehemently disagreed over whether to support the Fourteenth and Fifteenth Amendments, which expanded rights for African American men but did not explicitly advance women's equality.

Ultimately, the woman suffrage movement splintered into two groups in 1869: Elizabeth Cady Stanton and Susan B. Anthony's National Woman Suffrage Association (NWSA), which focused on a federal amendment enfranchising women, and Lucy Stone and Henry Blackwell's American Woman Suffrage Association (AWSA), which advocated a state-by-state effort to gain women the vote. The movement would remain divided for two decades.

"The right of citizens of the United States to vote shall not be denied or abridged by the United Sates or by any State on account of race, color, or previous condition of servitude."

—Fifteenth Amendment to the US Constitution, 1870

THE FIFTEENTH AMENDMENT.
CELEBRATED MAY 19ᵗʰ 1870

After emancipation, abolitionists sought political and civil rights for newly free African Americans. Wendell Phillips of the American Anti-Slavery Society discouraged a concurrent campaign for woman suffrage, arguing, "This hour belongs to the negro." Despite internal conflict, Phillips's strategy succeeded, and the Fifteenth Amendment, which prohibited states from using race as a barrier to the ballot box, was ratified in 1870. James C. Beard's 1870 lithograph, shown here, celebrates the Amendment.

I Sell the Shadow to Support the Substance.
SOJOURNER TRUTH.

Born into slavery, Sojourner Truth (ca. 1797–1883) became one of the abolition and women's rights movements' most commanding public speakers. At the 1867 AERA meeting, Truth declared, "if colored men get their rights, and no colored women theirs, you see the colored men will be masters over the women, and it will be just as bad as it was before." But Truth avoided suffrage movement politics and ultimately supported the Fifteenth Amendment. Truth sold *cartes-de-visite* like this one from 1864 to support herself, hence the message, "I sell the shadow to support the substance."

"I do not see how any one can pretend that there is the same urgency in giving the ballot to the woman as to the negro . . . With us, the matter is a question of life or death . . . When women, because they are women, are hunted down through the cities of New York and New Orleans; when they are dragged from their houses and hung upon lamp-posts; when their children are torn from their arms, and their brains dashed out upon the pavement; when she is an object of insult and outrage at every turn; when they are in danger of having their homes bur[n]t down over their heads; when their children are not allowed to enter schools, then she will have an urgency to obtain the ballot equal to our own."

—Frederick Douglass, speaking at the 1869 AERA meeting

At the formation of the AERA in 1866, poet and lecturer Frances Ellen Watkins Harper (1825–1911; pictured at right in 1898) observed the challenges of separating gender from race, saying, "You white women speak here of rights. I speak of wrongs. I, as a colored woman, have had in this country an education which has made me feel as if I were in the situation of Ishmael, my hand against every man, and every man's hand against me." A backer of the Fifteenth Amendment, Harper continued to work for woman suffrage as part of the AWSA and the Woman's Christian Temperance Union.

Elizabeth Cady Stanton and Susan B. Anthony (1820–1906; pictured left to right ca. 1875) opposed the Fifteenth Amendment because it did not enfranchise women simultaneously with African American men. When asked in 1867 if she would support black men getting the vote before women, Stanton replied, "I say no; I would not trust him with all my rights; degraded, oppressed himself, he would be more despotic with the governing power than even our Saxon rulers are." Preferring "educated suffrage" to male suffrage, Stanton and Anthony further fueled discord by touring with and accepting funding from racist entrepreneur George Francis Train to launch their newspaper *The Revolution*.

The Notorious Victoria Woodhull

Woodhull (pictured ca. 1871) used her newfound prominence in the suffrage movement to create a new political party, the Equal Rights Party, with Stanton, and in 1872 Woodhull ran for president of the United States, declaring Frederick Douglass her running mate (he never responded to the nomination). In 1884, lawyer Belva Lockwood also ran for president, rejecting suffrage leaders' appeals to support Republican presidential candidate James G. Blaine, maintaining instead that women needed their "own party."

A proponent of free love, spiritualism, vegetarianism, and other radical doctrines, Victoria Woodhull (1838–1927) was a bright but fleeting star of the suffrage movement. Woodhull and her sister ran the first woman-owned brokerage on Wall Street and used their profits to start a newspaper, *Woodhull and Claflin's Weekly*, with the bold motto—PROGRESS! FREE THOUGHT! UNTRAMMELED LIVES!—displayed atop each issue. In 1871 Woodhull became the first woman to speak in Congress on the subject of suffrage, arguing that women's right to vote was inherent in the Fourteenth and Fifteenth Amendments, which conferred citizenship upon all "persons" and protected those citizens' right to vote. Suffragists enthusiastically adopted the strategy.

After nationally prominent Congregational minister Henry Ward Beecher accused her of being a depraved sex radical, Woodhull retaliated by exposing in her newspaper his affair with a married Sunday school teacher. Woodhull was incarcerated for weeks for mailing the "obscene" newspaper. The resulting scandal embroiled the suffrage movement in a public relations disaster, and suffrage leaders distanced themselves from Woodhull.

As reported in *Frank Leslie's Illustrated Newspaper* (left), Woodhull lobbied the House Judiciary Committee on January 11, 1871, making the case that women's voting rights were protected by the Fourteenth and Fifteenth Amendments. In 1869, Missouri husband and wife Francis and Virginia Minor had articulated a similar legal strategy to establish women's right to vote without a new constitutional amendment, but Woodhull's notoriety brought the concept to the national stage.

Woodhull was maligned repeatedly in the press for her controversial beliefs. In this cartoon by Thomas Nast in the February 17, 1872, edition of *Harper's Weekly* (right), Woodhull is depicted as "Mrs. Satan" and holds a sign that reads, "Be saved by free love." A wife, carrying a heavy burden of children and drunk husband, says to her, "I'd rather travel the hardest path of matrimony than follow your footsteps."

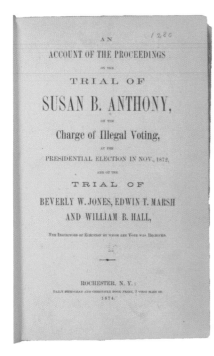

AN

ACCOUNT OF THE PROCEEDINGS

ON THE

TRIAL OF

SUSAN B. ANTHONY,

ON THE

Charge of Illegal Voting,

AT THE

PRESIDENTIAL ELECTION IN NOV., 1872,

AND OF THE

TRIAL OF

BEVERLY W. JONES, EDWIN T. MARSH

AND WILLIAM B. HALL,

THE INSPECTORS OF ELECTION BY WHOM HER VOTE WAS RECEIVED.

ROCHESTER, N. Y.:

DAILY DEMOCRAT AND CHRONICLE BOOK PRINT, 2 WEST MAIN ST.

1874.

Susan B. Anthony was arrested and stood trial for voting in Rochester, New York. The judge discharged the jury, summarily found her guilty, and levied a $100 fine for prosecution costs, which Anthony refused to pay. At her trial, an account of which was published in 1874 (above), Anthony invoked enslaved people who, seeking liberty, had gone "over, or under, or through the unjust forms of the law." She argued women must do the same to take their freedom: "I have taken mine, and mean to take it at every possible opportunity."

An Active Resistance to Tyranny

Numerous women, including Susan B. Anthony, attempted to vote in the 1872 federal election, bringing national attention to the grassroots efforts for women to obtain the vote by direct action. In 1869, Missouri suffragist Virginia Minor began advocating for women to go to the polls and sue if they were prohibited from voting, hoping to establish court rulings that validated women's right to vote under the Fourteenth and Fifteenth Amendments. When her own case, *Minor v. Happersett* (1875), reached the US Supreme Court, the Court ruled that citizenship did not guarantee the right to vote, defeating the whole strategy. Undeterred, Anthony and her fellow activists found new ways to disrupt social norms in their quest for voting rights, as Anthony proclaimed at her 1873 trial, "I shall earnestly and persistently continue to urge all women to the practical recognition of the old revolutionary maxim, that 'Resistance to tyranny is obedience to God.'"

On July 4, 1876, Susan B. Anthony and fellow members of the National Woman Suffrage Association interrupted the proceedings of the Centennial International Exposition in Philadelphia (right), taking the stage where Anthony addressed the crowd. The women distributed copies of their *Declaration of Rights of Women of the United States* (left) to attendees, including Vice President Thomas W. Ferry. When safely outside, Anthony read from the document, which called for "impeachment" to remove the word "male" from state laws that restricted voting rights.

"It was we, the people, not we, the white male citizens, nor yet we, the male citizens; but we, the whole people, who formed this Union. And we formed it, not to give the blessings of liberty, but to secure them; not to the half of ourselves and the half of our posterity, but to the whole people—women as well as men."

—*The Trial of Susan B. Anthony*, 1874

THE AGE OF BRASS.

or the triumphs of Womans rights

Suffragists' demand for the vote in increasingly public and disruptive ways exposed cultural anxiety over the challenge to traditional gender roles. Currier & Ives sent up this notion in *The Age of Brass. Or The Triumphs of Woman's Rights* (1869), in which "Celebrated Man Tamer" Susan Sharp-Tongue runs for office, supported by unfeminine women shown smoking cigars and threatening a man holding a baby.

Lifting as We Climb

A gifted orator, educator, and author, Hallie Quinn Brown (1849–1949; pictured ca. 1880) toured the country to raise money for Wilberforce University, her alma mater, and to speak about political causes, including civil rights, temperance, and woman suffrage. She was instrumental in the founding of the Colored Women's League of Washington, DC, the predecessor to the NACW.

In the late nineteenth century, increasing numbers of professional African American women formed civic and religious associations to work for the betterment of their communities. They fought to end racial discrimination and expand educational and economic opportunities in addition to seeking the right to vote. Many of these local clubs were united by the founding of the National Association of Colored Women (NACW) in 1896, with its motto, "Lifting as we climb."

At the same time, the two biggest and predominantly white suffrage organizations, NWSA and AWSA, merged to form the National American Woman Suffrage Association (NAWSA) in 1890. Believing they could not achieve nationwide suffrage without the support of Southern white women, leaders avoided the subject of race for fear of alienating those allies. Some, like Louisiana activist Kate M. Gordon, viewed woman suffrage as a tool for white supremacy. Though a few black women such as Mary Church Terrell were active in NAWSA, many others preferred to focus their efforts in their own organizations, free from prejudice.

"The Negro woman's club of to-day represents the new Negro with new powers of self-help, with new capacities, and with an intelligent insight into her own condition. . . . It means better schools, better homes and better family alignments, better opportunities for young colored men and women to earn a living, and purer social relationships."

—Fannie Barrier Williams, *The Colored American from Slavery to Honorable Citizenship*, 1902

Fannie Barrier Williams (1855–1944; pictured ca. 1885) successfully fought for African Americans' involvement in the 1893 Columbian Exposition in Chicago, where she delivered two lectures on the status of black citizens. A dedicated reformer, Williams saw women's clubs as one path to progress.

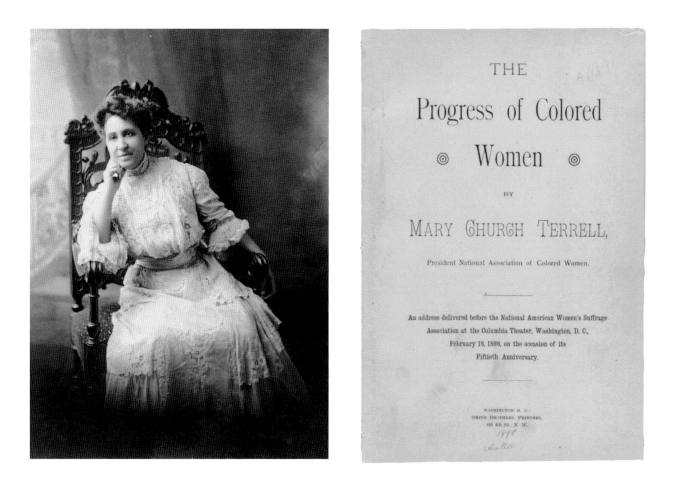

Lifelong civil rights advocate Mary Church Terrell (1863–1954; pictured at left ca. 1890) was the first president of the NACW and the first African American woman to serve on the Washington, DC, school board. When NAWSA invited Terrell to speak at their 1898 meeting (right), she emphasized the additional barriers faced by black women: "For, not only are colored women with ambition and aspiration handicapped on account of their sex, but they are everywhere baffled and mocked on account of their race . . . . Avocations opened and opportunities offered to their more favored sisters have been and are tonight closed and barred against them."

Temperance Tactics

The temperance movement, which focused on restricting or eliminating the drinking of alcohol, gained momentum throughout the nineteenth century, and women became an increasingly important voice in the cause. By 1900, the Woman's Christian Temperance Union (WCTU) had almost half a million members, while NAWSA claimed only 10,000 (that number increased to nearly 1,000,000 by 1915).

As with abolition, suffragists learned from the temperance campaign how to raise money, hold public meetings, conduct petition drives, and deal with hostile audiences. There was wide overlap between supporters of abolition, temperance, and women's rights; both Susan B. Anthony and Elizabeth Cady Stanton were active in the temperance movement before shifting their focus to suffrage. At a temperance convention in Rochester, New York, in April 1852, Stanton addressed nearly 500 people, calling for the total rejection of alcohol—"Let us touch not, taste not, handle not, the unclean thing"—and linked divorce reform to the need to protect wives and children from abusive "confirmed drunkards."

Temperance advocates viewed women as the primary victims of drunkenness and saw drinking as a gateway to all kinds of other societal ills, including gambling, adultery, and prostitution. Although women temperance advocates were essentially fighting for family values, ironically, participation in the temperance movement gave many their first experience of political activism, leading them out of the home and into meeting halls and leadership positions, which in turn led them to yearn for more rights.

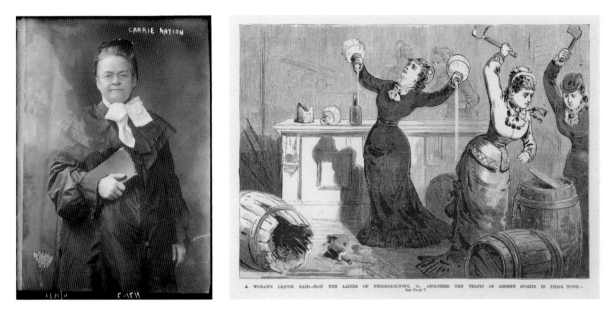

A WOMAN'S LIQUOR RAID—HOW THE LADIES OF FREDERICKTOWN, O., ABOLISHED THE TRAFIC OF ARDENT SPIRITS IN THEIR TOWN.—
SEE PAGE 7.

While many temperance supporters applied peaceful tactics, such as pleading with saloon owners to shutter their businesses or singing hymns outside of bars, "saloon-wrecker" Carrie Nation (1846–1911; left) and her followers took a more proactive approach, attacking saloons with a hatchet in the name of temperance—as pictured in *A Woman's Liquor Raid* in the November 8, 1879, issue of *The National Police Gazette* (right). Nation's violent assaults led to threats, beatings, and repeated jailings across across her home state of Kansas.

"I am a woman of destiny. I have been commissioned by the Almighty to save this nation from the curse of rum and tobacco. Look at my name on this little hatchet. 'Carrie A. Nation.' I am to carry this nation back to temperance."

—Carrie Nation, quoted in the *Boston Daily Globe*, August 29, 1902

In the latter half of the nineteenth century, women took on leadership roles in the temperance movement. The WCTU was founded in 1874 and Frances Willard (1839–1898; pictured below ca. 1890) became president five years later. She led the WCTU to adopt suffrage as part of their platform, arguing that women must have the right to vote in order to effect social change.

A SUGGESTION TO THE BUFFALO EXPOSITION.—LET US HAVE A CHAMBER OF FEMALE HORRORS.

This satirical cartoon, *A Suggestion to the Buffalo Exposition; Let Us Have a Chamber of Female Horrors*, by Louis Dalrymple (above) appeared in the April 3, 1901, issue of *Puck*. At the Buffalo World's Fair, Uncle Sam and John Bull take a group of world leaders through a center aisle between women representing a variety of "women's causes," of which both temperance and suffrage feature prominently. Among figures such as "Mrs. Faith Healer," "Woman Evangelist," "Mrs. Eddy Christian Scientist," and a woman labeled "D.A.R.," Susan B. Anthony and Elizabeth Cady Stanton (center left) are engaged in impassioned speech, former presidential candidate Belva Lockwood sits with her head in her hand (left side), and Carrie Nation (right side) holds her signature ax.

Victories out West

A leading suffragist in the Pacific Northwest, Abigail Scott Duniway (1834–1915; pictured ca. 1875) published the *New Northwest* out of Portland, Oregon, from 1871 to 1887. Duniway advertised her newspaper as "not a Woman's Rights, but a Human Rights organ, devoted to whatever policy may be necessary to secure the greatest good to the greatest number. It knows no sex, no politics, no religion, no party, no color, no creed." In 1871, Duniway toured the Northwest with Susan B. Anthony, traveling 2,000 miles and making sixty speeches.

Western territories and states were the first to welcome woman suffrage. Small territorial legislatures, the statehood process and ensuing state constitutional conventions, and a spirit of political experimentalism created unique environments that activists used to their advantage. Women in Utah Territory gained voting rights in 1870, but Congress disenfranchised them in an attempt to discourage the Mormon practice of polygamy in 1887. Only after the Mormon Church disavowed the custom in 1890 and Utah became a state in 1896 did women regain their right to vote.

Victories in Colorado (1893) and Idaho (1896) were won by referenda after the People's Party, a populist third party that represented the economic interests of farmers, assumed power. Not all efforts were successful. Referenda in South Dakota (1890) and California (1896) failed, as did one in Washington (1889)—even though as a territory Washington had enfranchised women in 1883.

In 1896, women in four states had full voting rights: Wyoming, Utah, Colorado, and Idaho. It would be another fourteen years before another state granted women the right to vote.

WOMAN SUFFRAGE IN WYOMING TERRITORY—SCENE AT THE POLLS IN CHEYENNE.

Wyoming's territorial legislature enfranchised women in 1869, supported by politicians who wished to raise the territory's profile and encourage women to move there, both to balance the majority-male population and to ensure white voters outnumbered Wyoming's growing African American population. In its November 24, 1888, issue, *Frank Leslie's Illustrated Newspaper* depicted women at the polls in Cheyenne, two years before the territory became a state.

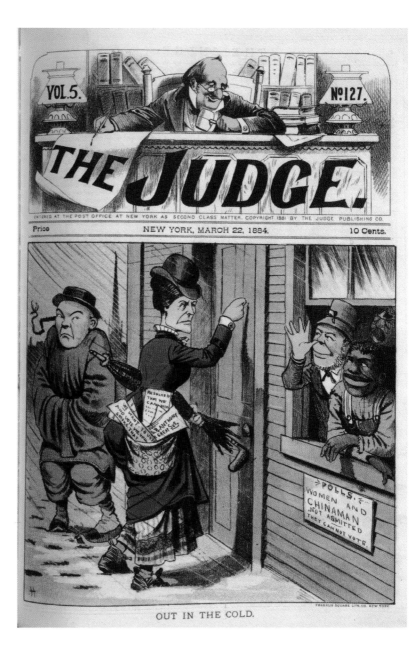

VOL.5. № 127.

THE JUDGE

ENTERED AT THE POST OFFICE AT NEW YORK AS SECOND CLASS MATTER. COPYRIGHT 1881 BY THE JUDGE PUBLISHING CO.

Price | NEW YORK, MARCH 22, 1884. | 10 Cents.

POLLS.
WOMEN AND
CHINAMAN
NOT ADMITTED
THEY CANNOT VOTE.

FRANKLIN SQUARE LITH. CO. NEW YORK

OUT IN THE COLD.

Grant E. Hamilton's cover for *Judge* (March 22, 1884) employs gross stereotypes to depict the two groups left "out in the cold" at the polls—women and Chinese immigrants—while enfranchised Irish and African American men observe them from inside. Anti-Chinese prejudice was widespread in the West, and suffragists used the specter of Chinese voters to argue for white women's voting rights. In 1882, the Chinese Exclusion Act severely limited immigration and barred Chinese Americans from becoming naturalized citizens, curtailing their voting power.

Chapter 2

NEW TACTICS FOR A NEW GENERATION

The new century demanded new approaches to gain women's voting rights. With increasing educational and professional opportunities, women's role in American society was shifting outside the domestic sphere, a change that both energized suffrage supporters and antagonized their opponents. The National American Woman Suffrage Association (NAWSA), led first by Carrie Chapman Catt and then by Dr. Anna Howard Shaw, remained the principal suffrage organization during this era, opening national headquarters on Fifth Avenue in Manhattan. Smaller local and special interest groups also proliferated. Many suffragists turned their attention overseas, watching British activists undertake militant protests and conferring with other reformers at international gatherings.

The suffrage debate entered the mainstream political discourse in the first decades of the twentieth century, spurred by high-profile public demonstrations and victories in Western states. In a vibrant age for print culture, suffrage organizations large and small produced newsletters, broadsides, and pamphlets, while the media covered the movement with cartoons, magazine covers, and illustrations, leaving a lively visual record of the campaign's increasing urgency.

Rea Irvin, *We Want Our Rights*, published as the cover for *Life*, February 20, 1913 (detail).

Deeds, Not Words

In 1903, British activist Emmeline Pankhurst founded the Women's Social and Political Union (WSPU) with the motto "Deeds, not words" to confront and pressure politicians into granting women the vote. WSPU members organized open-air assemblies, held massive parades, and disrupted politicians' public meetings. Many were arrested and imprisoned, with some enduring force-feeding while on hunger strikes. Such militant tactics raised the profile of the suffrage movement, as Pankhurst acknowledged in her autobiography, *My Own Story* (1914): "Our heckling campaign made women's suffrage a matter of news—it had never been that before. Now the newspapers were full of us."

Along with her daughters, Christabel and Sylvia, Pankhurst forced traditional suffrage organizations such as Millicent Fawcett's National Union of Women's Suffrage Societies to adopt these new methods. British suffragists were not the only ones watching, as American women debated whether and how much to emulate their comrades across the Atlantic.

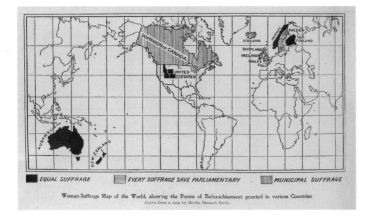

EQUAL SUFFRAGE   EVERY SUFFRAGE SAVE PARLIAMENTARY   MUNICIPAL SUFFRAGE

Woman-Suffrage Map of the World, showing the Forms of Enfranchisement granted in various Countries
Drawn from a map by Bertha Damaris Knobe

Americans took note of suffrage victories around the world, as depicted in Bertha Damaris Knobe's map for *Harper's Weekly* from April 25, 1908. Knobe's accompanying article previewed the 1908 meeting of the International Woman's Suffrage Alliance, a group led by Carrie Chapman Catt with many American and British members.

When Emmeline Pankhurst (1858–1928) first toured the United States in 1909, the *Woman's Journal* wrote, "There is no woman in England today who is so hated and feared by the politicians, or who is regarded with intense enthusiasm and devotion by so many women." Pankhurst was welcomed back in 1911 (seen at right in New York) and 1913 (a ticket for one of her lectures seen below), although as the WSPU's tactics became more controversial, including destroying property, so did her presence among American suffragists.

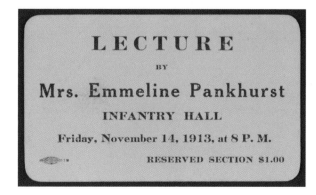

LECTURE

BY

Mrs. Emmeline Pankhurst

INFANTRY HALL

Friday, November 14, 1913, at 8 P. M.

RESERVED SECTION $1.00

"The more they repress us, the more heavily they punish us, the more they fire our indignation, the more determined they make us to get the vote for women, if it costs life itself."

—Christabel Pankhurst, Emmeline Pankhurst's daughter, in *The Militant Methods of the NWSPU*, 1908

Recognizing the power of compelling imagery to influence public opinion, the Artists' Suffrage League in Britain created posters, postcards, banners, and other visual materials for the movement. Duncan Grant was a joint winner in one of the League's poster competitions with this 1909 entry, *Handicapped!* which illustrates the ease with which men sail with the vote, while women struggle to row choppy waters without it. In America, the *Woman's Journal* sold this and other British posters for 25 cents each, stating, "Every Suffrage Club which has Headquarters needs at least one of these posters on its walls."

The New Woman

Access to education and professional careers, and work in support of reform movements, including the fight for the vote, combined to create a novel social type by the turn of the twentieth century: The New Woman. She was young, beautiful, educated, cultured, and athletic, representing an aspirational ideal of white, upper-middle-class American womanhood. For some, these new concepts of femininity represented a threat to the social order, and anxiety about changing gender roles played out in posters, magazine illustrations, and other cultural expressions of the age.

Poking fun at reversed gender roles in this 1901 stereograph, a New Woman wearing knickers and smoking a cigarette assesses a man, likely her husband, who labors over the laundry tub on washday.

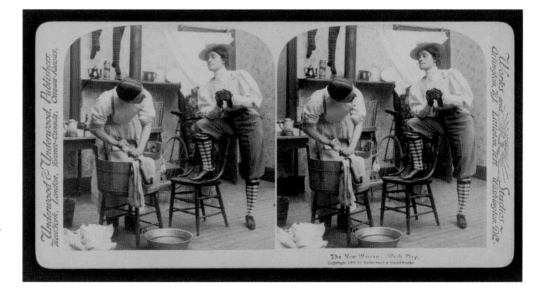

Known as "Gibson Girls," Charles Dana Gibson's depictions of active and engaged young women became synonymous with the idea of the New Woman. Gibson Girls were tall, slender, and fashionably dressed, with an iconic pompadour hairstyle. In this 1895 poster for *Scribner's Magazine* (left), a Gibson girl participates in one of the decade's biggest fads: riding a bicycle.

With *In the Political Equality Nursery* (1912, right), published in *Life* magazine, Laura Foster imagined one ramification of women gaining the vote: men would be responsible for childcare. Crying children overwhelm the apron-wearing men in the cartoon, originally captioned with a play on the traditional nursery rhyme: "Bye, Baby Bunting, / Mother's gone to meeting, / Gone to get her ballot in."

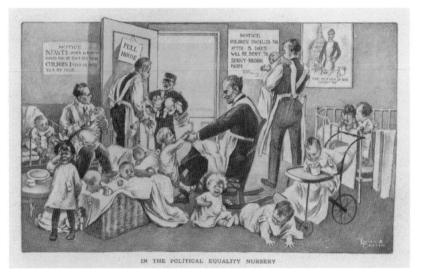

IN THE POLITICAL EQUALITY NURSERY

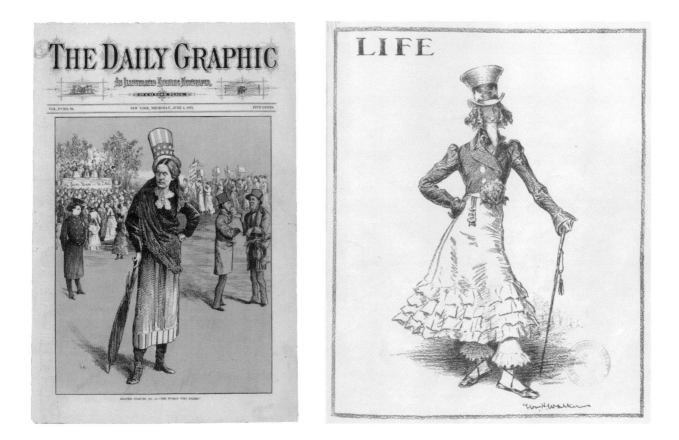

Created more than forty years apart, these two cover illustrations employ remarkably similar imagery to convey the ongoing discomfort with women's changing place in society. In 1873, Thomas Wust depicted Susan B. Anthony as *The Woman Who Dared* for *The Daily Graphic* (left). Anthony, wearing a star-spangled top hat, defiantly poses before a man holding a baby and a crowd of women holding banners aloft. William H. Walker's gender-bending Uncle Sam shows off his bloomers and petticoats in *Equal Suffrage*, a cover for *Life* in 1914 (right).

Gentlemen Stand for Suffrage

Although the suffrage movement was driven by women, some men were sympathetic to the cause from the beginning. Early supporters included William Lloyd Garrison, Ralph Waldo Emerson, and Frederick Douglass. Between 1874 and 1875, a Young Men's Woman Suffrage League met regularly in New York City and in 1909, 150 or so men met in editor Max Eastman's Greenwich Village apartment to form the Men's League for Woman Suffrage. Initially the idea was for prominent men to lend their names to the cause, and League members quickly embraced their role and began speaking, writing articles and editorials, and lobbying legislators. Additional chapters sprung up nationally, and by 1917—when the vote was won in New York State—membership was in the thousands across thirty-five states. The men's positions of influence yielded beneficial press and gave them access to important legislators, including President Woodrow Wilson.

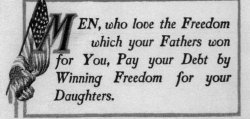

MEN, who love the Freedom which your Fathers won for You, Pay your Debt by Winning Freedom for your Daughters.

In their suffrage scrapbooks from the years 1910 and 1911, Elizabeth and Anne Miller recognized the importance of men's efforts in "Winning Freedom for Your Daughters," particularly documenting the work of their friends Max Eastman and Nathaniel Schmidt in organizing the Men's League for Woman Suffrage of the State of New York. George Foster Peabody, William Dean Howells, and John Dewey were among other prominent charter members.

SAINT GEORGE AND THE DRAGON

On Wednesday, February 22d, the anti-suffragists, at the hearing in the Assembly Chamber at Albany, made an attack upon the women voters of Colorado. Exactly forty-eight hours later Judge Ben B. Lindsay stood in the same Assembly Chamber and, in a counter-attack of two hours, beat to the ground every false statement.

This 1911 *Votes for Women Broadside* cartoon by Martha Bryn celebrates Colorado judge Ben B. Lindsay for slaying the dragon of Falsehood, Prejudice, and Misrepresentation. At a hearing on proposed legislation that would enfranchise women in New York State, Judge Lindsay skewered anti-suffragists' arguments by sticking up for the women voters of Colorado after they had been maligned by suffrage opponents.

The Company of Men in the Procession.
(Photos by the Pictorial News Co.)

During a 1911 suffrage parade in New York City, the eighty-nine men who marched with the Men's Suffrage League were subjected to cries of "Hold up your skirts, girls!" and other jeers. This photograph (left) appeared in a news article and was preserved by the Millers in their suffrage scrapbooks.

Robert Cameron Beadle (1883–? pictured at right, holding his hat in the air) became a member of the Men's League through his close associate George Foster Peabody and eventually took over the role of secretary from Max Eastman. His various activities in supporting suffrage included performing a vaudeville sketch, donning an Uncle Sam costume, and riding horseback from New York City to Washington, DC, to demand a constitutional amendment. Next to Beadle is Alfred H. Brown, another League member, pictured in 1913.

Winning Them Over

Suffragists and their supporters made their case for women's voting rights with a range of arguments in a variety of media, especially in newspapers, magazines, broadsides, and pamphlets. Bold typography and eye-catching illustrations drew readers in and provided a platform for activists to make their case. Motherhood and the moralizing influence of women on politics were popular themes. Some works depicted other groups that could or could not vote—in both cases, comparing them unfavorably to an idealized educated white woman and displaying common prejudices of the era.

Lou Rogers, a rare woman cartoonist in the early twentieth century, took a more cynical attitude to the question of how women's votes would influence society in her drawing for *Judge* (February 8, 1913). In *From Force of Habit She Will Clean This Up*, a woman armed with apron, bucket, and broom faces "the municipal ballot" marred by cobwebs and grime labeled with social ills, including "the sweatshop." Rogers, who created many pro-suffrage illustrations and served as art director for Margaret Sanger's *Birth Control Review*, questioned whether the moral influence of women was more an obligation than a noble cause.

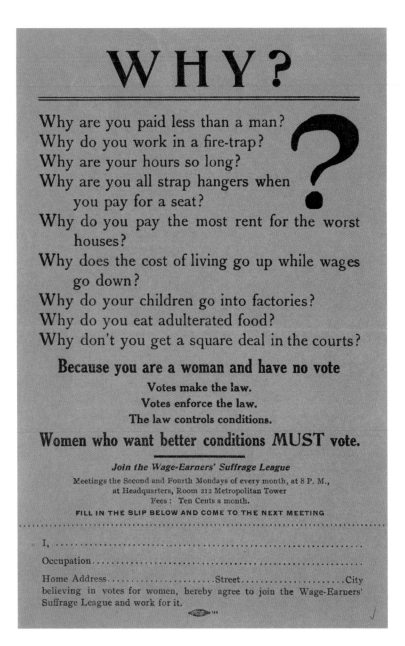

WHY?

Why are you paid less than a man?
Why do you work in a fire-trap?
Why are your hours so long?
Why are you all strap hangers when
    you pay for a seat?
Why do you pay the most rent for the worst
    houses?
Why does the cost of living go up while wages
    go down?
Why do your children go into factories?
Why do you eat adulterated food?
Why don't you get a square deal in the courts?

Because you are a woman and have no vote

Votes make the law.
Votes enforce the law.
The law controls conditions.

Women who want better conditions MUST vote.

Join the Wage-Earners' Suffrage League

Meetings the Second and Fourth Mondays of every month, at 8 P. M.,
at Headquarters, Room 212 Metropolitan Tower
Fees : Ten Cents a month.

FILL IN THE SLIP BELOW AND COME TO THE NEXT MEETING

I,..

Occupation..

Home Address......................Street......................City
believing in votes for women, hereby agree to join the Wage-Earners'
Suffrage League and work for it.

This broadside, published by the Wage-Earners' Suffrage League, targeted working women with a series of direct questions about labor and living conditions. The answer to all the questions is simple: "Because you are a woman and have no vote."

Kansan suffragist Henrietta Briggs-Wall commissioned W. A. Ford to create *American Woman and Her Political Peers* (1893), depicting WCTU leader Frances Willard surrounded by exaggerated stereotypes of other disenfranchised groups: "idiots, convicts, the insane, and Indians" (1911 postcard edition, left). Orson Lowell used the opposite conceit for his *Life* cover (1913, right). The title's *Four Voters*—caricatures of an African American, a laborer, an aesthete, and a gangster—stand around an elegant woman dressed all in white, the only member of the group without the vote.

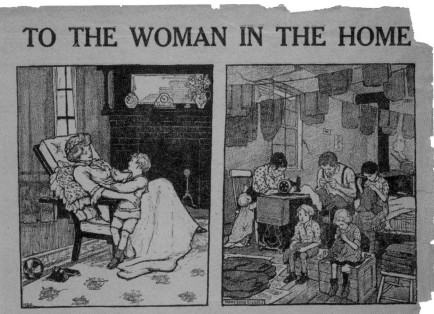

TO THE WOMAN IN THE HOME

How can a mother rest content with this—   When such conditions exist as this?

There are thousands of children working in sweat-shops like the one in the picture. There are thousands of children working in mines and mills and factories. Thousands more are being wronged and cheated by Society in countless ways.

IS NOT THIS **YOUR** BUSINESS?

Intelligent citizens WHO CARED could change all this—providing always, of course, that they had the power of the ballot.

DO **YOU** CARE?

Mothers are responsible for the welfare of children. This duty as mothers requires that they should demand

VOTES FOR WOMEN!

NATIONAL WOMAN SUFFRAGE PUBLISHING CO., Inc.

PUBLISHERS FOR THE

NATIONAL AMERICAN WOMAN SUFFRAGE ASSOCIATION
505 FIFTH AVENUE   NEW YORK CITY

Addressed "To the Woman in the Home," this NAWSA broadside (ca. 1913, with a sketch by Mary Ellen Sigsbee) charged middle-class women, like the one on the left, with the responsibility for eradicating child labor, as depicted on the right. "Mothers are responsible for the welfare of children. This duty as mothers requires that they should demand votes for women!"

James Montgomery Flagg used imagery of motherhood on his cover for the October 27, 1917, issue of the *Woman Citizen*, which replaced NAWSA's *Woman's Journal* that same year. A woman cradles an infant above the slogan, "Women Bring All Voters Into the World. Let Women Vote."

Organized Opposition

In the nineteenth century suffragists struggled to be taken seriously. During the first-ever vote on a federal woman suffrage amendment in January 1887 (the bill had first been introduced in 1878) only fifty of seventy-six senators even bothered to vote. Major opponents included Midwestern liquor interests, Southern conservatives who wanted to protect their region's de facto disenfranchisement of black men, and Eastern business leaders who relied on child labor and unregulated working conditions. Many people—male and female—feared that voting rights would overburden women and threaten families and that women's lack of political knowledge would weaken the government. Satirical cartoons abounded, mocking the emotional, impressionable, and frivolous nature of women.

Perhaps surprisingly, most anti-suffrage organizations were founded and led by women. While female anti-suffragists, called "remonstrants" and later "antis," began organizing locally as early as the 1860s, anti-suffrage activity revved up around the turn of the century, especially in the Northeast. In 1911, the National Association Opposed to Woman Suffrage formed with Josephine Dodge at the helm. Anti-suffrage groups adopted tactics similar to those of their pro-suffrage counterparts, writing articles, distributing newsletters, posters, and leaflets, making speeches, and appearing before congressional committees or in other forums.

Founded in 1911—the same year this photograph (above) was taken by DC-based photography firm Harris and Ewing—the National Association Opposed to Woman Suffrage distributed a newsletter, the *Woman's Protest*, and organized events and state campaigns.

Suffragists were often portrayed as masculine, unattractive, and sometimes even dangerous and unhinged. Published in an 1892 edition of *Puck*, Udo J. Keppler's illustration, titled *The Feminine of Jekyll and Hyde* (right), shows a woman holding a flag labeled "Woman Suffrage" standing behind an angry hag labeled "Militant Lawlessness" rushing toward the viewer, carrying a bomb and a torch labeled "Arson."

THE FEMININE OF JEKYLL AND HYDE.

America When Femininized

"SET ON THEM YOURSELF, OLD MAN, MY COUNTRY CALLS ME!"

"WHY, MA, THESE EGGS WILL GET ALL COLD!"

SUFFRAGIST—FEMINIST IDEAL FAMILY LIFE.

The More a Politician Allows Himself to be Henpecked
The More Henpecking We Will Have in Politics.

A Vote for Federal Suffrage is a Vote for Organized Female
Nagging Forever.

In this drawing by James Montgomery Flagg that appeared in a 1907 edition of *Harper's Weekly* (below), the American women in this apparently peaceful protest are incongruously labeled "suffragettes," the term used to describe British women who used militant and sometimes violent tactics to make their case. An anonymous "anti" wrote in the September 1912 edition of the *Woman's Protest*, "It is more exciting to attend suffrage meetings, speak to street crowds, walk in parades, and easier to believe in the fallacy that the vote will change all the evils of the world, than it is to give hours, days, thought, and energy to quiet, persistent, unheralded work toward the amelioration of the condition of women, children, and the unfortunate. The vote never has accomplished, and never will accomplish, all this."

Antis subscribed to the traditional belief that an orderly society depended on women maintaining the domestic sphere while men engaged in the public sphere. This broadside, produced by the Southern Woman's League for Rejection of the Susan B. Anthony Amendment (above), explains, "Woman Suffrage . . . masculinizes women and feminizes men" and shows a cartoon of a hen with a Votes for Women sash telling a befuddled rooster to sit on the nest of eggs himself.

THE AMERICAN SUFFRAGETTES

No Central Strategy

National suffrage leaders faced competing and sometimes conflicting demands by regional organizations that constrained their ability to advance one message. Southern suffragists advocated for states' rights to determine voting laws and used racist arguments in favor of voting rights for educated white women. At the same time, progressive politics brought victories in seven Western states between 1910 and 1915, which fueled momentum toward a federal amendment.

California Campaign Edition

THE WESTERN WOMAN VOTER

VOL. 1   SEATTLE, WASHINGTON, SEPTEMBER, 1911   NO. 9

COLLEGE GIRLS PUTTING UP SUFFRAGE POSTERS

WASHINGTON, last November, gave women the ballot by 20,000 majority---the largest majority ever given a suffrage amendment in the history of the world. Here's to a bigger majority in California on October 10!

California Next ! !

Seattle suffragists launched the *Western Woman Voter* to serve as a resource for newly enfranchised women in Washington after the state granted women the right to vote in 1910. This September 1911 issue looked ahead to California's referendum the following month.

THE AWAKENING

By 1915, women had full voting rights in eleven Western states. Henry Mayer showed women clamoring for their rights as progress moved eastward in this illustration, *The Awakening*, for *Puck* (February 20, 1915).

"It is to the strong, courageous, and progressive men of the Western States that the women of this whole country are looking for deliverance . . . It is these men who must start this movement and give it such momentum that it will roll irresistibly on to the very shores of the Atlantic Ocean."

—Ida Husted Harper, *Women's Tribune*, July 8, 1905

Methodist minister and doctor Anna Howard Shaw (1847–1919; pictured at left in 1914) tried to avoid conflicts over race while serving as president of NAWSA from 1904 to 1915. Shaw refused to sanction explicitly whites-only suffrage campaigns in the South, writing in 1906 to NAWSA's Business Committee that it could not "be allied with any movement which advocated the exclusion of any race or class from the right of suffrage." When National Association for the Advancement of Colored People president W. E. B. Du Bois criticized NAWSA's failure to endorse the fight for African American voting rights as a shared cause with woman suffrage, Shaw invited him to address NAWSA's 1912 convention.

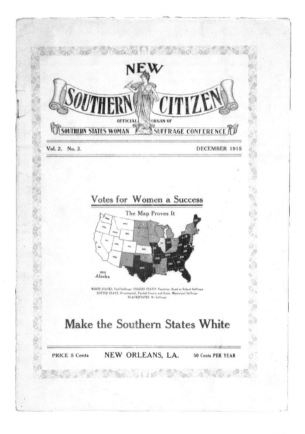

In 1913, former NAWSA corresponding secretary Kate M. Gordon founded the Southern States Woman Suffrage Conference to emphasize the sovereignty of states to determine their own voting laws—enabling the continued suppression of the African American vote in the South. The use of "white" to connote enfranchisement created a racist double-entendre on the December 1915 cover of the Conference's publication, the *New Southern Citizen*: "Make the Southern States White" (right).

Songs of Suffrage

Its mocking tone notwithstanding, this lively lithographed illustration on the cover of Frank Howard's 1869 anti-suffrage song demonstrates that pro-suffrage leaders had become household names. The cover shows a group of women, children in tow, voting under banners that read "Vote for Susan B. Anthony for President," "Governor of Mass Lucy Stone," "Gov. of New York Elizabeth Cady Stanton," "Down with Male Rule," and "Vote Early and Often."

From local meetings to citywide marches, suffragists consistently asserted their unbreakable spirit in song. Many suffrage songs featured original texts sung to well-known tunes, such as "Yankee Doodle" and "America." On June 15, 1911, the *New York Times* published a story about suffragists in Los Angeles who were informed by police that "votes for women" speeches were prohibited at the rally. To circumvent the ordinance, the suffragists set their speeches to music and sang their messages instead. Suffrage organizations across the country sponsored song competitions encouraging activists of both sexes to pen music for the movement.

Song was also used by the anti-suffragists at rallies, and anti-suffrage sentiment seeped into much of the popular music of the time. Sheet music cover art depicts frazzled and emasculated men relegated to the kitchen, laundry, or nursery, surrounded by screaming, fighting, and hungry children, while the woman of the house waltzes out the door to vote.

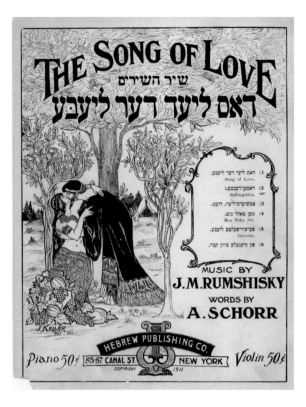

This Yiddish sheet music published in 1911 for "Damen Rechte" ("Women's Rights," translated as "Suffragettes" on the sheet music) by Joseph Rumshinsky and Anshel Schorr (left) not only advocates for women's right to vote, but for equal opportunities in many roles, including soldier, politician, and rabbi.

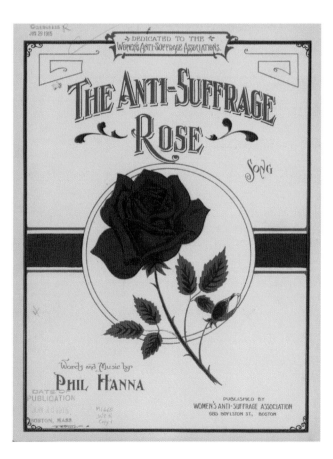

Phil Hanna's 1915 song, "The Anti-Suffrage Rose" (right), published by the Women's Anti-Suffrage Association of Massachusetts, was well known among anti-suffragists and was often featured at rallies and fairs. The song asserts that the rose, the official flower of the anti-suffragists, is far sweeter and superior to the yellow jonquil, a symbol of the suffrage movement: "Lovely Anti-Suffrage Rose. / You're the flow'r that's best of all! / You're better far, than jonquils are, / We are going to prove it in the Fall."

A good example of popular music of the day, this song advanced one of the most convincing arguments to persuade men (and some women) that women deserved the right and responsibility to vote. Published in 1916, this upbeat song was probably intended to be played and sung at home to entertain and perhaps gently persuade.

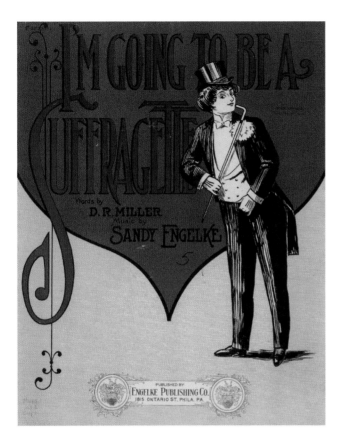

In D. R. Miller's "I'm Going to Be a Suffragette" (1910, left), the image of a suffragist dressed like a man illustrates the common anti-suffrage belief that voting would masculinize women. In the lyrics, a husband ridicules his wife's newfound political interest. She responds in the refrain, "I'm goin' to be a suffragette, Billy / Hear me shout Hurray, Hurray. / Now don't you think that I am silly / or will waste my time away. / The sex that always joggled the cradle / have got some rights you bet. / I say Hip Hip Hip Hip Hip Hurray / I'm goin' to be a suffragette."

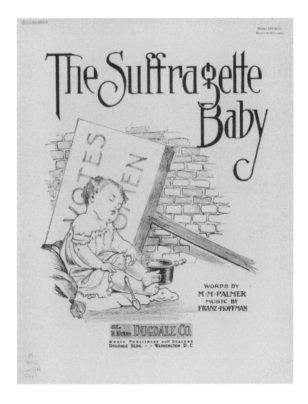

A common argument against woman suffrage, reflected in the cover of the sheet music for Franz Hoffman's 1913 song "The Suffragette Baby" (right), was that voting women would neglect their domestic duties.

The Most Conspicuous and Important Demonstration

In late 1912, Alice Paul and Lucy Burns sought appointment on NAWSA's lethargic congressional committee. Both women had recently been involved in the militant suffrage movement in England and had met in jail after they were arrested at a demonstration. Within months, Paul, Burns, and their recruits had organized a massive national suffrage parade in the nation's capital, modeled on the elaborate pageants held in Britain and local marches in New York. The event was scheduled for the day preceding President Woodrow Wilson's inauguration to ensure maximum press attention.

According to a NAWSA broadside, the parade was "the most conspicuous and important demonstration that has ever been attempted by suffragists in this country." The parade received wide publicity, not only for its costumes, floats, and colorful tableaus, but also for the failure of the Washington, DC, police to control the crowds of men who gathered to watch.

On February 12, with cameras clicking, sixteen "Washington hikers" left New York City to walk to Washington for the parade. Led by "General" Rosalie Jones (1883–1978), the procession included a yellow horse-drawn suffrage cart filled with leaflets and buttons, which they distributed along the route, engaging whenever possible with the local media. The New York State Woman Suffrage Association's journal crowed that "no propaganda work undertaken by the State Association and the Party has ever achieved such publicity."

The dramatic flair of the program's cover (left) shows vividly the organizers' intent to frame the march as a momentous event. Artist Benjamin M. Dale employed recurring motifs of the American suffrage movement—the herald sounding a horn, the motto "Votes for Women," and the colors purple, gold, and white. Such imagery was easily recognized by the general public and served as unifying symbols for those within the suffrage movement.

Mirroring the cover of the program, lawyer Inez Milholland (1886–1916, right) rode as the first of four mounted heralds. Behind Milholland stretched nine bands, four mounted brigades, three heralds, more than twenty floats, and some 5,000 marchers. Women from countries that had already enfranchised women held the place of honor in the first section of the procession. Then came the "Pioneers" who had been struggling for decades to secure women's right to vote. The next sections celebrated working women, grouped by occupation. The state delegations followed, and finally the section for male supporters.

When the procession reached the Treasury Building, one hundred women and children presented an allegorical tableau written especially for the event to show "those ideals toward which both men and women have been struggling through the ages and toward which, in co-operation and equality, they will continue to strive." The *New York Times* described the pageant as "one of the most impressively beautiful spectacles ever staged in this country." At right, German actress Hedwig Reicher wears the costume of "Columbia."

IDA B. WELLS.

Although Paul initially discouraged black women from participating for fear of losing Southern white women's involvement, she received pushback, including from Anna Howard Shaw, who wrote to Paul to "instruct all marshalls to see that all colored women who wish to march shall be accorded every service given to other marchers." Organizers concocted a plan whereby men's suffrage leagues would separate white and black women participants. Accounts of what actually transpired differ. Many black suffragists were segregated, but not all. Notably Ida B. Wells-Barnett (1862–1931, pictured at left in 1891), fearless journalist, anti-lynching crusader, and founder of the Alpha Suffrage Club for African American women, marched with her state contingent from Illinois, despite some of them endorsing the parade's official segregated stance.

The parade elicited wide coverage in the press, mainly due to the inaction of the police as crowds of rowdy and inebriated men cursed, threatened, and mobbed the women before a cavalry unit restored order. Public outcry over the ill treatment of the march participants led to a congressional investigation, the removal of the police chief, and "indignation meetings" staged throughout the country. Even NAWSA officials, leery of Alice Paul's affiliation with militant British suffragettes, conceded that the police debacle solidified support among "those who were wavering" and brought "to our ranks thousands of others who would never have taken any interest."

Chapter 3

FORTITUDE, SACRIFICE, VICTORY

Suffrage propaganda and ephemera saturated the country during the 1910s, appearing in everything from songs, movies, and food products to dolls and postcards. While leaders of the newly formed Congressional Union (CU), later the National Woman's Party (NWP), focused on public protests in Washington, DC, officials of the National American Woman Suffrage Association (NAWSA) unveiled their "winning plan," which coordinated state work with more aggressive lobbying in the nation's capital. By the end of 1916, both NAWSA and the NWP were working toward a federal amendment—but through very different methods.

When the United States entered World War I, many suffragists stopped campaigning for the vote and devoted themselves to war work. The NWP, however, did not halt its protests, a decision many considered treasonous. Beginning in June 1917, picketing suffragists were arrested, imprisoned, and subjected to brutal treatment. Women from all social classes risked their health and reputations by continuing to protest for the vote.

Finally, in 1919, the years of struggle and sacrifice began to pay off: the House passed the suffrage amendment on May 21, and the Senate followed suit on June 4. Victory was in reach, but it would take another fourteen months of hard work to win the amendment's ratification.

NWP members picketing against President Woodrow Wilson in Chicago, October 19, 1916.

Provocative Protest

Harriot Stanton Blatch and Alice Paul each brought militant protest tactics developed in Britain to their home country. Blatch—Elizabeth Cady Stanton's daughter—inherited the mantle of suffrage leadership upon her return to the United States after two decades in Britain. Alice Paul's homecoming in 1910 was covered in the American press, which had followed her imprisonment and force-feeding in London. Blatch and Paul bucked the conservative leadership of NAWSA, encouraging provocative demonstrations that took women out of their traditional domestic domain and onto the front pages of newspapers. Paul argued that the movement should focus on a federal amendment rather than NAWSA's state-by-state strategy, and in time, Blatch agreed. In 1916, Blatch's Women's Political Union merged with Paul's Congressional Union (CU).

When Harriot Stanton Blatch (1858–1940, pictured at left ca. 1913) returned to New York after living in England for two decades, she found that the American suffrage movement "bored its adherents and repelled its opponents." Seeking to revitalize the cause, Blatch established the Equality League of Self-Supporting Women in 1907, a group designed to build solidarity between working class and professional women while advocating for suffrage in New York State. The League was renamed the Women's Political Union in 1910. Blatch was a politically savvy strategist who promoted publicity-generating protests as well as lobbying.

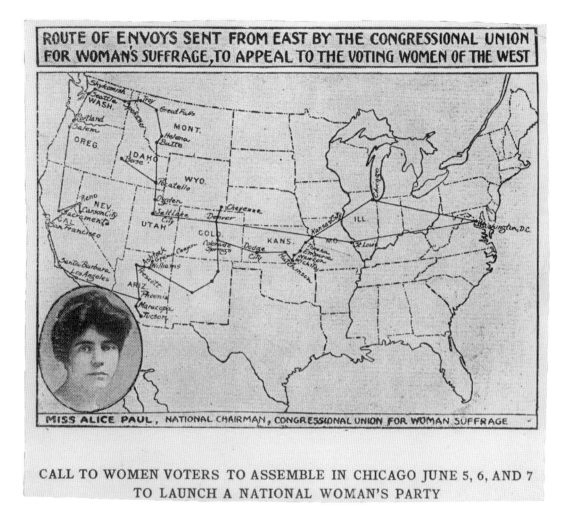

ROUTE OF ENVOYS SENT FROM EAST BY THE CONGRESSIONAL UNION FOR WOMAN'S SUFFRAGE, TO APPEAL TO THE VOTING WOMEN OF THE WEST

MISS ALICE PAUL, NATIONAL CHAIRMAN, CONGRESSIONAL UNION FOR WOMAN SUFFRAGE

CALL TO WOMEN VOTERS TO ASSEMBLE IN CHICAGO JUNE 5, 6, AND 7 TO LAUNCH A NATIONAL WOMAN'S PARTY

Alice Paul (1885–1977) founded the CU in 1913 with Lucy Burns, fellow veteran of the British suffrage campaign, to fight for voting rights using the techniques they learned abroad. As advertised in the above map, the CU convened in Chicago in 1916 to create the Woman's Party, dedicated solely to advocating for a federal suffrage amendment in states that had already enfranchised women. Borrowing another practice from the Pankhursts, Paul encouraged supporters to hold the political party in power responsible for lack of progress toward suffrage, engaging in partisan activity that NAWSA disdained. The Woman's Party and the CU merged to form the National Woman's Party in March 1917.

The CU began publishing the weekly newsletter *The Suffragist* in November 1913 and the paper quickly attracted 1,200 paid subscribers. In this July 1916 photograph, Frances Pepper (left) and Elizabeth Smith (right) are seen in the weekly's offices. The newsletter ceased publication shortly after suffrage was achieved and relaunched in 1923 under its new name, *Equal Rights*.

"There is no other issue comparable in importance to the elementary question of self-government for the women of America."

—Alice Paul, in the first issue of *The Suffragist*, November 15, 1913

Marketing the Movement

Between 1886 and 1920 American suffragists published at least six cookbooks to raise money, attract members, and dispel fears that enfranchised women would shirk domestic responsibilities. Advertisements for this 1915 cookbook published by the Equal Franchise Federation of Western Pennsylvania offered the reassuring tagline "The Best Cooks Are Suffragists," with cover art showing a calm Uncle Sam holding the sexes in balance while twelve states and Alaska granted women full or partial (Illinois) suffrage. Recipes were contributed by group members and well-known literary and political figures.

During the last decade of the suffrage campaign, greater mass production of commercial goods combined with new marketing techniques created an environment that both suffragists and manufacturers profitably exploited. Mainstream and militant suffragists alike saturated the marketplace with a proliferation of suffrage commodities, available especially in major urban centers but also through catalog sales. These included badges, pins, clothing, playing cards, dolls, tea sets, fans, food, and more. In addition, women opened suffrage restaurants, grocery stores, and retail shops; produced suffrage movies, plays, and songs; and unleashed an unprecedented stream of political print culture. Through their pervasiveness, these suffrage-themed products helped to legitimize the movement, advance its "political salesmanship," raise money, and keep the cause ever-present in daily life.

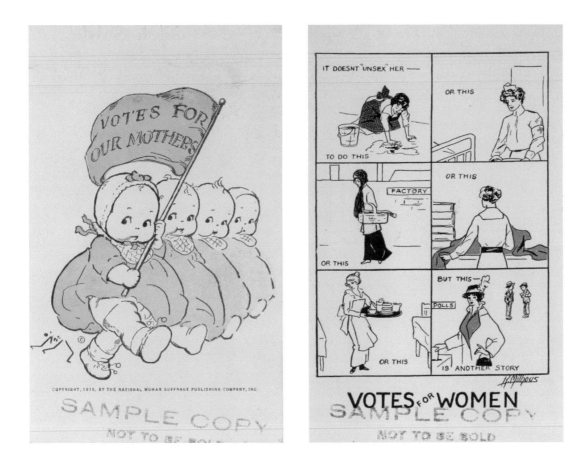

NAWSA sold a large supply of suffrage merchandise, particularly postcards bought in bulk by local groups. These were advertised in suffrage periodicals but also in a widely distributed catalog and price list. Popular cards included anything by feminist artist Rose O'Neill featuring her beloved "Kewpie" characters (left) and Katherine Milhous's cartoon (right) exposing hypocritical arguments that voting would "unsex" women.

Cincinnati artist Lillian E. Whitteker designed this doll pattern in 1914 (right), possibly as part of the nation's spontaneous Buy-a-Bale movement, intended to ease the calamitous drop in cotton prices caused by the wartime disruption of American exports to Europe. Attempting to curry favor for suffrage in the South, Anna Howard Shaw sent $50 checks to fourteen of NAWSA's state associations to buy bales of cotton. Simultaneously she urged Southern textile manufacturers to eliminate child labor, adding a touch of irony to the Little Suffragist Doll.

Although fund-raising "suffrage teas" were more common, coffee drinkers also supported suffrage coffee houses and attended coffee socials. Both beverage products were packaged with suffrage labels and sold in stores. In 1916, Florence Livingston Lent of the Massachusetts Woman Suffrage Association began advertising Suffrage Fund Coffee in issues of the *Woman's Journal* (left). Distribution quickly extended to other states, including Rhode Island, where prominent suffragist Sara M. Algeo became the product's principal agent.

KEEP COOL!

There will be nothing to worry about after we get

VOTES FOR WOMEN

Election Day | November 2

New York State Woman
Suffrage Association

Some suffrage novelties, such as this fan from the Empire State Campaign of 1915 (left), were intended as free souvenirs for parade watchers, petition signers, or passersby pausing for a street lecture. Although defeated at the polls in November, New York suffragists had gamely distributed more than twenty tons of leaflets, 1,000,000 buttons, 200,000 matchbooks, and 35,000 "Keep Cool" fans, 500 of which were eagerly snatched up by bankers and brokers during "Wall Street Day" demonstrations on September 15.

Votes
for Women Ball
Grand Central Palace Feb 16 at 8PM
Tickets for Sale at Women's Political Union
25 West 45th Street
50 cents

Despite skepticism from other suffrage organizations, the Women's Political Union held its first "Votes for Women Ball," in February 1912 at Murray Hill Lyceum in New York City. At just 50 cents a ticket, the fundraiser aimed to be inclusive, and it drew nearly 2,000 dancers, including striking garment workers admitted free of charge. This flyer is for the February 1915 ball (right), held in the considerably larger Grand Central Palace on Park Avenue, for which 15,000 tickets were sold.

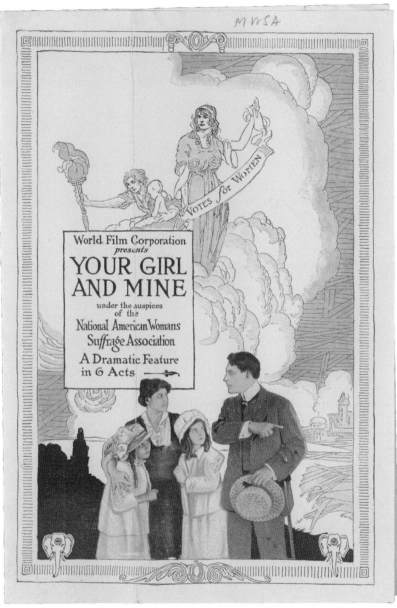

Many early motion picture films depicted suffragists as pathetic spinsters or aggressive shrews who neglected their homes, browbeat their husbands, and ignored their children. In response, suffragists began making their own films portraying themselves as crusaders devoted to their families and to fighting political corruption. The 1914 melodrama *Your Girl and Mine*, produced by suffrage lobbyist and future congresswoman Ruth Hanna McCormick, revolves around Rosalie Fairlie, a young bride who suffers under laws unfavorable to women.

Into the Streets

Inspired by British militancy and the international labor movement, suffragists used transcontinental auto trips, speaking tours, mass meetings, banners, and billboards to bring their cause to the public, and they encouraged other civic and religious organizations to embrace their campaign.

The first American suffrage parade took place in February 1908, when twenty-three women marched in New York City, followed by parades later that year in Iowa and California. Over the next few years, participation swelled, especially in New York, with 20,000 people marching in November 1912. Prevailing notions about middle-class femininity dictated that virtuous

Nannie Helen Burroughs (1879–1961; pictured at far left ca. 1910) fought for voting rights as an officer of the Woman's Convention, an auxiliary of the National Baptist Convention that united many African American congregations and supported social reforms. Burroughs advocated for suffrage specifically to empower black women, writing in *The Crisis* in 1915, "When the ballot is put into the hands of the American woman the world is going to get a correct estimate of the Negro woman. It will find her a tower of strength of which poets have never sung, orators have never spoken, and scholars have never written."

In 1914, Alice Paul's Congressional Union planned a "Mayday from ocean to ocean," in which women in cities across the country held local meetings and parades on May 2 demanding a federal suffrage amendment. Three days later, the House Judiciary Committee set the stage for both houses of Congress to vote on just such an amendment. On May 9, suffragists convened in Washington, DC, to march to the US Capitol and demand the vote, but Congress did not act. The procession is shown here at the Capitol steps.

women should not be seen walking the streets. By intentionally crossing this boundary with their highly organized and theatrical processions, suffragists attracted notice from the public, politicians, and the press—all of whom they needed to advance their cause.

Some activists feared such provocative acts were too divisive. Looking back, Carrie Chapman Catt provided perspective in *Woman Suffrage and Politics* (1923): "New York women were deliberately doing the ridiculous thing in order to challenge men's attention and so make men think. The campaign of 1915 thus kept itself before the public on the plane of the public every hour of every day."

A Boston newspaper described activist Margaret Foley in 1911, "she stands five feet eight and weighs in at one hundred and forty, but she can easily manage seven feet, turn her brown hair to flame, descend like a mountain of brick and extend her mellifluous accent to megaphonics." No stranger to spectacle, Foley was known for heckling politicians at public meetings, and in 1910 she distributed suffrage flyers from a hot air balloon. Here, Foley addresses a crowd in Cleveland, Ohio, in May 1912.

"What could be more stirring than hundreds of women, carrying banners, marching—marching—marching!"

—Harriot Stanton Blatch in her memoir, *Challenging Years*, 1940

In 1911, Caroline Lexow asserted in the British suffrage journal *The Vote*, "Every cause needs its picture. We must have demonstrations that impress the eye." To this end, participants in New York's May 4, 1912, suffrage parade (left) were instructed to wear white "for best effect." The event attracted 10,000 marchers, and that number would double at a parade that fall.

In 1915, the Women's Political Union ran a horse-drawn "suffrage van" (right) to facilitate impromptu street speeches and meetings. The *New York Tribune* called the van "gorgeous in its coat of purple, white and green, with 'Votes for women' lettered all over it, even on its roof." On its inaugural journey from Brooklyn to City Hall Park, the van was led by a horse called Votes.

Silent Sentinels

The protesters called themselves "Silent Sentinels" because they stood without speaking as a gesture of strength and restraint. The idea was proposed by Harriot Stanton Blatch, who had employed a similar tactic in 1912 at the New York State legislature. Here, Alison Turnbull Hopkins pickets at the White House on New Jersey Day, January 30, 1917.

After President Wilson's reelection, Alice Paul called for members of the NWP to picket the White House. Daily picketing began on January 10, 1917, with Paul and a group of twelve women holding banners demanding an amendment. During that year, nearly 2,000 women from across the country joined the picket line outside the White House.

Initially, protesters stood silently, holding placards inscribed with relatively tame messages such as "Mr. President, what will you do for Woman Suffrage?" President Wilson maintained decorum, greeting the protesters with a tip of the hat as he rode through the White House gates. But the mood changed when the United States entered World War I on April 6. The picketers brandished more provocative placards that pointed out the hypocrisy of fighting for democracy abroad when women could not vote at home. Crowds grew angry and hurled insults and rotten fruit at the protesters, sometimes pushing them to the ground and ripping or stealing their banners. Often, the police simply watched without acting.

To maintain interest in the press, Alice Paul and Lucy Burns organized groups representing women from different regions and walks of life to picket on different days. Here, women from Pennsylvania stand on the picket line on January 24, 1917.

Carrying banners representing their state, profession, or local suffrage organization, women assembled on March 4, 1917, for the Grand Picket, when more than 1,000 suffragists marched around the White House for several hours in an icy, driving rain, waiting in vain to present a series of resolutions to President Wilson on the eve of his second inauguration (right).

The picketers endured through cold and rain, keeping warm with hot chocolate, fur coats, and wooden boards and hot bricks on which to stand (left). A January 12, 1917, article in the *Washington Herald* described their determination: "The wintry blasts turned their lips blue, and continuous shivering was in order, but, according to the pickets, it will take more than the icy hands of winter to drive them from their posts."

Jailed for Freedom

A friend of Alice Paul from their days in the British movement, Lucy Burns (1879–1966) was instrumental in founding the CU and planning the White House pickets. Burns was arrested and imprisoned six times, enduring solitary confinement and force-feeding. This photograph was likely taken while Burns was imprisoned at the Occoquan Workhouse in November 1917.

The White House tolerated the pickets until June 22, 1917, when Lucy Burns and Katherine Morey were arrested, ostensibly for obstructing traffic. Police warned that future picketers would face the same penalties, but Alice Paul insisted the NWP protests were legal. For several weeks, picketers were arrested, refused to pay their fines, and served a few days in prison. As summer stretched into fall, angry, often violent crowds gathered around the protesters, incensed at what they considered unpatriotic messages on the suffragists' banners. When arrested, picketers faced longer prison sentences of sixty days to six months, to be served at the Occoquan Workhouse in Virginia instead of the District jail.

Suffrage prisoners endured unsanitary conditions and contaminated food. On the "Night of Terror," November 14, 1917, Occoquan guards beat the picketers, knocking one woman unconscious. When prisoners began hunger strikes, they were brutally force-fed. Alice Paul was threatened with transfer to an institution for the insane.

The harsh treatment of the prisoners became its own story, turning public opinion in favor of the suffragists. Though a federal appeals court declared the picketers' arrests unconstitutional in March 1918, police continued to arrest women protesting at the US Capitol, the White House, and Lafayette Park over the next two years. By the end of the campaign, 168 NWP members had served time in prison or jail.

On June 20, 1917, Lucy Burns, Katherine Morey (both pictured above, left to right), and Dora Lewis stood outside the White House during a visit from Russian officials, America's allies in World War I. Their banner read, in part: "President Wilson and Envoy [Elihu] Root are deceiving Russia. They say we are a democracy . . . We, the women of America, tell you that America is not a democracy." Angry passersby, incensed by the suffragists' message during wartime, destroyed the banner, as seen at bottom. Burns and Morey were arrested when they returned to picket two days later.

As prison sentences for picketers lengthened in the fall of 1917, Alice Paul joined the fray. On October 20, she left NWP headquarters for the White House with a banner emblazoned with President Wilson's own words (right): "The time has come to conquer or submit for there is but one choice. We have made it." Paul was arrested and sentenced to seven months in prison. She initiated a hunger strike, as she had done in England. Prison staff forced a tube down her throat and poured in milk and eggs three times each day until Paul and the other protesters were released on November 23.

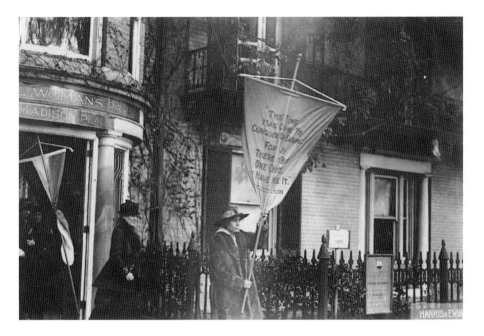

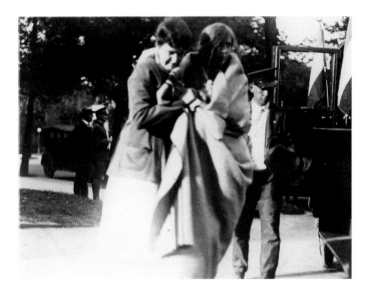

Most picketers were educated, white, upper- and middle-class women, making their arrests and treatment more shocking to the public. Whether or not they engaged in hunger strikes, the women suffered from undernourishment and foul conditions while incarcerated, emerging ill or severely weakened. At left, art student Kate Heffelfinger leaves Occoquan Workhouse, where she had been sentenced to six months imprisonment. Heffelfinger would be arrested twice more at NWP protests.

The suffragists' poor treatment in prison sparked further protests. The NWP insisted that the picketers should be considered political prisoners since their punishment far exceeded their crime of "obstructing traffic." Mary Winsor, who was herself arrested twice for picketing, carried this banner in 1917 (left).

Affidavit of Mrs. Minnie P. Quay.

I arrived at Occoquan on the evening of Nov. 14th, 1917, after waiting about an hour in the office of the Work House, The Supt. Mr. Whittaker arrived with about thirty guards, suddenly seized all of our party and dragged us out of the room into the darkness across the road some distance and threw us into a dark dirty dungeon. The dungeon I was in was very filthy, tobacco spit on the floor all along the side of the filthy bunk Dirty horse blankets open dirty toilet, no water, dark and damp. I was so cold my teeth chattied all night. Supt. Whittaker ran up and down the corridor screaming to the guards to bring the handcuffs straight jacket and gags, threatening to put them on Miss Julia Emory who was in the dungeon with me. Then opened the door of the dungeon Miss Lucy Burns was in pulled her hands thru the bars and handcuffed them. The next morning I was taken to Supt. Whittakers office. He informed me he had a Whipping Post at Occoquan, and that he used it on the prisioners. He then sent me over to the men's hospital where I remained for ten days. The first three days I was feed on bread and filthy milk, and something in it tast like carbolic acid.

Minnie P. Quay

This affidavit by Minnie P. Quay (right) describes the prisoners' treatment on the "Night of Terror" at Occoquan Workhouse.

The NWP took full advantage of the publicity generated by the arrests, organizing a cross-country "Prison Special" tour in 1919 featuring women who had served time for protesting. Lucy Branham, arrested for picketing in 1917, addressed a crowd wearing her drab "prison costume."

"We are put out of jail as we were put in—at the whim of the government. They tried to terrorize and suppress us. They could not, so they freed us."

—Alice Paul upon her release from prison, November 23, 1917

85

Wartime Measures

NWP member Virginia Arnold holds a banner accusing President Wilson of hypocrisy. When a similar banner was first displayed in August 1917, an angry mob attacked the picketers and destroyed the banner while police did little to intervene.

When the United States declared war on the German Empire on April 6, 1917, suffragists were divided about how to respond. The NWP continued its picket of the White House. But most suffragists felt they should shelve their activism in favor of war work and hoped their efforts would be rewarded with the vote. Indeed, many countries around the world had adopted woman suffrage since the war's start, including Canada, Russia, Norway, Finland, and Denmark.

Women all over the country—suffragists and antis alike—threw themselves into the war effort. On the home front they stepped into jobs vacated by men, worked in munitions factories and other defense industry jobs, and led efforts to produce and conserve food. Abroad, they labored as nurses, translators, mechanics, telephone operators, ambulance drivers, and myriad other roles, often working close to the front lines and enduring extreme living conditions. Their wartime service helped convince many legislators—including President Wilson himself—that women did deserve the vote.

Carrie Chapman Catt's presidential address—framed as an address to Congress—was the highlight of NAWSA's 49th annual convention in December 1917. In it, she referenced the ongoing war: "The world tragedy of our day is not now being waged over the assassination of an archduke, nor commercial competition, nor national ambitions, nor the freedom of the seas. It is a death grapple between the forces which deny and those which uphold the truths of the Declaration of Independence." The published speech (left) shows a soldier telling Uncle Sam to extend democracy to women. NAWSA sent copies to all Congressmen and state legislators.

The Red Cross began sending nurses to Europe even before the United States entered the war. By the war's end, more than 20,000 American nurses had served. Kenneth Russell Chamberlain's cartoon *The Weaker Sex?*, published in *Puck* in November 1914 (right), highlights the courage of these nurses, who routinely braved the front lines of battle to aid wounded soldiers, risking injury and illness.

C. D. Batchelor's cartoon on the cover of the December 28, 1918, edition of the *Woman Citizen* calls attention to the many contributions of women to the war effort.

Boardman Robinson's May 16, 1913, cartoon for the *New York Tribune* depicts a familiar experience for suffrage lobbyists: a senator waves a polite farewell while hiding the "US Senate Committee Report on Woman Suffrage" behind his back. Two days before the cartoon was published, the *New York Times* stated that the Senate Committee on Woman Suffrage reported favorably on a federal suffrage amendment, but "there is little likelihood that the resolution will be considered by either house at this session. If it came to a vote it would be overwhelmingly rejected."

Lobbying Lawmakers

While some suffragists built awareness through public demonstrations and media attention, others dedicated their efforts to political lobbying. Both NAWSA and the NWP engaged in lobbying with one key difference: the NWP campaigned against Democrats, who controlled Congress and the White House, while the NAWSA remained staunchly nonpartisan. Both advocated for a federal suffrage amendment, which, after it was rejected in 1887, continued to be introduced in every Congress until 1919. State victories, even if incremental, helped build momentum for federal action: in 1917 alone, municipal, primary, or presidential suffrage was enacted in six states, with New York granting full voting rights to women.

Carrie Chapman Catt (1859–1947) reluctantly assumed a second term as NAWSA president in 1915. Since 1904, when her previous term concluded, Catt had traveled the world as president of the International Woman Suffrage Alliance and organized a suffrage campaign in New York State. Under Catt's leadership, NAWSA instituted a hierarchical structure for local societies, creating "suffrage schools" to teach women around the country how to organize. When the United States entered World War I, Catt encouraged NAWSA members to contribute to the war effort, compromising her personal pacifist beliefs while winning appreciation from the Wilson administration.

"Woman are not in rebellion against men. They are in rebellion against worn-out traditions."

—Carrie Chapman Catt, speaking to the Federation of Women's Clubs, Chicago, 1914

Catt unveiled her "winning plan" at the NAWSA convention in Atlantic City in September 1916: pursuit of a federal suffrage amendment through coordinated state campaigns. The campaigns would support full suffrage referenda in states where success was likely, and seek incremental suffrage in others, with the ultimate goal of increasing support for change at the federal level. This cover of the *NAWSA Headquarters Newsletter* from August 15, 1916 (left), contrasts Catt's plan with "detours" represented by other strategies: "State Action," preferred by Southern suffragists, because it privileged states' rights, and "Federal Action," preferred by the militant NWP.

Suffragists gained a valuable ally in Congress in 1916 when Jeannette Rankin (1880–1973; shown at right ca. 1917) became the first woman elected to the US Congress. A Republican from Montana, Rankin was a NAWSA field secretary who had worked on multiple Western state suffrage campaigns. In the House, Rankin helped form the Woman Suffrage Committee and advocated for the federal suffrage amendment. Rankin lost her 1918 senate campaign and worked for pacifist causes before winning reelection to the House in 1940.

The Tide Turns

VOL. LXXVII No. 25

Wilson Out For Federal Amendment On Suffrage

Women Have Earned Right to Ballot in War, He Says

400 Votes in House Expected To-day

Victory for the Anthony Amendment in Senate to Follow, Is Belief

By James Arthur Seavey

WASHINGTON, Jan. 9.—President Wilson to-day gave his indorsement to Federal woman suffrage. The President told House leaders this afternoon that he favored passage of the Susan B. Anthony suffrage amendment, which comes up for a vote in the House to-morrow.

The Republican members of the House met in caucus at the Capitol to-night, and late in the session Representative Mondell, of Wyoming, introduced a resolution to the effect that it be the sense of the caucus that all the members support the suffrage amendment. Enemies of the amendment tried immediately to get a nadjournment and failed. Then a motion to table the Mondell resolution was defeated.

As reported in the *New York Tribune*, President Wilson announced his support for the suffrage amendment in January 1918.

As the decade neared its end, government officials found it increasingly difficult to deny women the vote, as they were contributing so much to the war effort. Anti-suffragist arguments about the mental and physical inferiority of women were impossible to sustain as women took over jobs vacated by men drafted into military service. The radical shock tactics of the NWP and public support for its imprisoned members, combined with NAWSA's persistent lobbying, eventually won President Wilson's endorsement of the Nineteenth Amendment, which was passed by the House of Representatives in January 1918. Obstructionists from Southern and Eastern states delayed passage in the Senate, while suffragists continued to lobby, picket, protest, and keep watch fires burning in front of the White House. The amendment passed the House again in May 1919, and by June the Senate, now with a Republican majority, passed it by a vote of 66 to 30, two more than the two-thirds required. The victory was massive, but the job was far from complete. The amendment would need to be ratified by thirty-six states.

Suffragists claimed a huge victory when women won the vote in New York State in 1917. A petition signed by more than 1,000,000 women signaled their determination to gain the vote. In this image by the National Photo Company (below), three New Yorkers exercise their newfound right.

In January 1918, President Wilson addressed Congress, "We have made partners of women in this war . . . Shall we admit them only to partnership of suffering and sacrifice and toil and not to a partnership of privilege and right?" Although Wilson, shown above in 1919, had begun his first term opposed to suffrage, his stance softened under political pressure and in recognition of women's substantial efforts to support the United States in World War I. Women voters had also played a crucial role in his 1916 presidential reelection: that year, women could vote in twelve states, eleven of which went to Wilson.

Clifford Berryman's cartoon *Votes for Women Bandwagon*, published in the *Evening Star* on January 10, 1918 (left), signaled the turning of the tide as congressmen began to announce their support for woman suffrage.

Even as the passage of suffrage seemed inevitable, the NWP continued their relentless pressure. In January 1919, members began gathering to burn copies of the president's speeches about democracy in urns outside public buildings, including the White House. These "Watchfires of Freedom" (right) resulted in more arrests and provoked numerous counter demonstrations.

Suffrage Won—Forward, March!

Immediately after Senate passage of the Nineteenth Amendment—also known as the Susan B. Anthony Amendment—Carrie Chapman Catt sent telegrams to state governors urging a quick ratification process and mobilized NAWSA's ratification committees in each state. Within four months, seventeen states had ratified the amendment, but victory could not be claimed until another nineteen states approved the measure. By the fall, Catt felt the need to embark on a "Wake Up America" tour, holding conventions and meeting with state officials in thirteen states over eight weeks. When the amendment was still unratified at the time of the Democratic and Republican political conventions in June 1920, the NWP sent delegations to both, lobbying holdout states and asking the parties to add support for suffrage into their platforms. The Democrats agreed to the suffrage plank, but Republicans did not, and the NWP responded by picketing their convention.

Finally, after fourteen long months, Tennessee became the thirty-sixth state to ratify the Nineteenth Amendment. On August 26, Secretary of State Bainbridge Colby signed the amendment into law, giving some 27,000,000 American women the right to vote.

Shown below at the Republican Convention in Chicago in June 1920, members of the NWP carried banners for Tennessee and Connecticut and a large sign accusing the Republican Party of defeating ratification of the Nineteenth Amendment in Delaware and blocking its ratification in Vermont and Connecticut. (Left to right, Abby Scott Baker, Eleanor Taylor Marsh, Sue White, Elsie Hill, and Betty Gram.)

Suffrage activists who had worked for years to secure the right to vote were invited to witness governors signing the amendment. Above, supporters wearing "Votes for Women" sashes watch as Governor Edwin P. Morrow of Kentucky signs the Anthony Amendment on January 6, 1920. Kentucky was the twenty-fourth state to ratify the amendment.

As each state voted for ratification, Alice Paul and members of the NWP sewed a star on their ratification flag, emulating the founding mother Betsy Ross. Upon receiving word that Tennessee had voted to ratify, Paul unfurled the ratification flag with thirty-six stars from the balcony of NWP headquarters in Washington, DC (left).

When Carrie Chapman Catt arrived in New York on August 27, 1920, she received a victory bouquet of flowers from Mrs. John Blair and was greeted by Governor Al Smith, Senator William M. Calder, Mary Garrett Hay, Mrs. Arthur Livermore, Harriet Taylor Upton, and Marjorie Shuler (right).

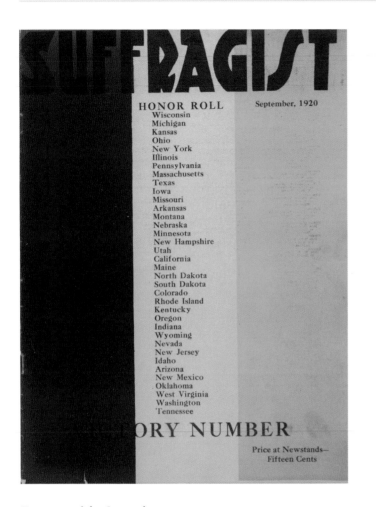

SUFFRAGIST

HONOR ROLL   September, 1920
Wisconsin
Michigan
Kansas
Ohio
New York
Illinois
Pennsylvania
Massachusetts
Texas
Iowa
Missouri
Arkansas
Montana
Nebraska
Minnesota
New Hampshire
Utah
California
Maine
North Dakota
South Dakota
Colorado
Rhode Island
Kentucky
Oregon
Indiana
Wyoming
Nevada
New Jersey
Idaho
Arizona
New Mexico
Oklahoma
West Virginia
Washington
Tennessee

ORY NUMBER

Price at Newstands—
Fifteen Cents

"The right of citizens of the United States to vote shall not be denied or abridged by the United States or by any State on account of sex."

—Nineteenth Amendment to the US Constitution, 1920

The cover of the September 1920 issue of *The Suffragist* (above) replicated the tricolor suffrage banner with the names of the thirty-six states in the order that they ratified the Nineteenth Amendment.

NAWSA celebrated the passage of the Nineteenth Amendment with this enthusiastic and patriotic cover by C. D. Batchelor in the December 4, 1920, issue of its publication, the *Woman Citizen* (opposite).

THE Woman Citizen

THE WOMAN'S JOURNAL FOUNDED 1870

TEN CENTS A COPY

DECEMBER 4, 1920

SUFFRAGE WON—FORWARD, MARCH!

Chapter 4

THE FIGHT CONTINUES

Ratification of the Nineteenth Amendment capped a seven-decade quest to win voting rights for women. While there was much to celebrate, suffrage leaders understood the struggle for full equality was not over. The National American Woman Suffrage Association (NAWSA) was superseded by the League of Women Voters, while the National Woman's Party (NWP) turned its attentions to legislative measures protecting and extending women's rights.

Many women did not immediately reap the benefits of the Nineteenth Amendment, as African Americans, Native Americans, and others faced state and federal regulations that barred their admittance to the full rights of citizenship. For the next century, women continued to fight for expanded access to the ballot box and true equality before the law. They are still fighting.

"Women who have taken part in the long struggle for freedom feel today the full relief of the victory. Freedom has come not as a gift but as a triumph, and it is therefore a spiritual as well as political freedom which women receive."

—Alice Paul, June 4, 1919

Liza Donovan, *Hear Our Voice*, 2017 (detail).

Now What?

Even before the Nineteenth Amendment had passed the House and Senate, NAWSA leader Carrie Chapman Catt began planning a League of Women Voters to educate women about political processes and influence policy, while remaining strictly nonpartisan. When the new organization was officially formed in 1920, Chapman handed the reigns to president Maud Wood Park. Alice Paul remained at the helm of the NWP, which regrouped to focus on passing a federal Equal Rights Amendment (ERA)—drafted by Paul and first introduced in Congress in December 1923—as well as other legislation to support equal rights for women.

Politicians courted their new constituents and women's organizations around the country held mock elections where women could practice voting. But despite these varied efforts, women failed to vote in large numbers. A study undertaken to understand the reasons women refrained from voting in the 1923 Chicago mayoral election uncovered a variety of reasons, including indifference, opposition to woman suffrage, and the objections of their husbands. It was not until 1980 that women turned out to the polls in equal proportion to men.

In the 1920s the League of Women Voters sponsored "Get Out the Vote" campaigns. Here, a group of members pose with their signs in September 1924.

Members of the Colorado branch gathered with NWP organizers Margaret Whittemore and Mabel Vernon around the back of a car with the banner, "National Woman's Party Women for Congress Campaign Coast to Coast Tour" in Colorado Springs in April 1926 (above). The NWP launched two major "Women for Congress" campaigns in 1924 and 1926. (Left to right: Norma W. Dodge, Katherine Courtney, Lillian H. Kerr, Bertha W. Fowler, Margaret Whittemore, Mrs. Lawrence T. Grey, Mabel Vernon, Rowena Dashwood Graves, Caroline E. Spencer, Ernestine Parsons, Eva Shannon.)

Despite encouragement to exercise their civic duty—as seen in this cartoon by William Stephen Warren that likely appeared in the *Cleveland News* (right)—women failed to vote in large numbers after ratification of the Nineteenth Amendment.

Expanding the Right to Vote

Obstacles to voting continued after the Nineteenth Amendment was ratified, but so did campaigns to tear them down. In an October 27, 1920,
letter, Mary Church Terrell declared herself "the first victim after the
Ratification of the Nineteenth Amendment north of the Mason & Dixon
Line" when a train ticket agent arrested her for "disorderly conduct" after she had inquired about an African American organizer for the Republican Party in Dover, Delaware. Terrell continued, "The colored women of
the South will be shamefully treated, and will not be allowed to vote, I am
sure. . . . We are so helpless without the right of citizenship in that section of the country where we need it most." Ostensibly protected by the
Fourteenth and Fifteenth Amendments, African Americans were sys-
tematically prevented from voting throughout the South until the civil
rights movement successfully pressed for reforms in the 1960s.

Native Americans and certain immigrant groups also faced barriers
to citizenship that prevented them from voting. Though some tribes
and individuals had been granted citizenship previously, not all Native
Americans were considered citizens until 1924. As during the woman
suffrage movement, service during wartime, changing social mores, and
persistent political pressure all buoyed activists toward expansions of
the franchise, reaching toward true universal suffrage.

In 1943, the US wartime alliance with China prompted Congress to reverse the Chinese Exclusion Act (1882). The Magnuson Act made Chinese Americans eligible for citizenship, and therefore, to vote. The *Gila News-Courier* reported on the bill to its audience (above), thousands of Japanese Americans forcibly detained at the Gila River internment camp in Arizona during World War II. Naturalization restrictions on other Asian immigrants, including Japanese, were not overturned fully until 1952.

Ratified in 1971, the Twenty-sixth Amendment lowered the voting age from twenty-one to eighteen. The military draft age had been similarly lowered during World War II, and as controversy over conscription during the Vietnam War grew, "old enough to fight, old enough to vote" became a rallying cry for those in favor of enfranchising eighteen- to twenty-year olds. Once the amendment passed, groups such as Frontlash's Youth Vote Project targeted new voters to encourage registration, as seen in this 1971 poster at right.

After years of protest and lobbying by African Americans and their supporters, the Voting Rights Act became law on August 6, 1965, prohibiting measures designed to prevent them from voting and empowering the Department of Justice to monitor elections for discriminatory practices. In his cartoon, *Continuation of a March* (below), published five days after the law was enacted, Herbert Block shows black voters lining up to vote, continuing their long fight for equality.

African Americans faced significant barriers to voting, as state and local governments placed a series of restrictions on voter registration, including poll taxes and literacy tests. Civil rights organizations such as the National Association for the Advancement of Colored People (NAACP) viewed voting rights as crucial to protecting black Americans from discrimination and racial violence. Elton C. Fax created this poster, *Finish the Fight* (above), for the NAACP in 1946.

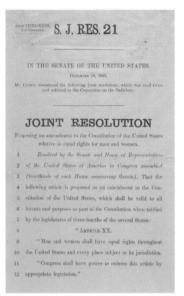

S. J. RES. 21

IN THE SENATE OF THE UNITED STATES.

JOINT RESOLUTION

Alice Paul drafted the Equal Rights Amendment (ERA) as early as 1921, and it was first introduced in Congress on December 10, 1923 (above, Senate Joint Resolution 21). It was introduced in every session of Congress for forty-nine consecutive years, with slight revisions to the wording. Many former suffragists opposed the amendment, fearing it would invalidate labor regulations designed to protect women. In 1972, both the House and Senate passed the amendment and it went to the states for ratification. Thirty-five states ratified the amendment before the 1982 deadline, three short of the needed thirty-eight.

Voting Is Not Enough

Armed with the vote, women continued to expand their political power and press for equality. The NWP lobbied for legislation that would benefit women, including enabling women to keep their US citizenship if they married citizens of other countries—as was the case with men—and repealing the regulation that prohibited working for the federal government if one's spouse was also a federal employee. One of their signature projects was an Equal Rights Amendment (ERA) to ban all forms of sex discrimination.

As the women's liberation movement took hold in the 1970s, the ERA—first introduced in 1923— gained renewed support. Women sought parity in all aspects of life, whether political, professional, social, or domestic. Increasing numbers of women entered realms previously closed to them, including the highest levels of government. Activists used protest tactics developed during the suffrage movement in their ongoing fight for full equality.

"Equality of rights under the law shall not be denied or abridged by the United States or any State on account of sex."

—The Equal Rights Amendment, as proposed in 1972

Women outside the Capitol demonstrated their support for the ERA in 1979, drawing specific connections to the protest tactics of the suffragists by wearing white and carrying tricolor banners, as captured in this photograph by Bettye Lane.

BRING U.S. TOGETHER

VOTE **CHISHOLM** 1972

UNBOUGHT AND UNBOSSED

Shirley Chisholm (1924–2005) was the first African American woman elected to Congress, where she represented New York's 12th District in the House from 1969 to 1983. A Democrat, she ran for president in 1972, the first black woman to seek a major party's nomination. Chisholm's campaign slogan, "Unbought and Unbossed," featured on this 1972 poster (left), characterized her forceful advocacy for her constituents.

Sandra Day O'Connor (born 1930) was the first woman to serve on the US Supreme Court, nominated by President Ronald Reagan in 1981 and confirmed unanimously. O'Connor commanded significant power as a moderate conservative and swing vote during her years on the bench, retiring in 2006. Courtroom artist Marilyn Church drew O'Connor being sworn in as associate justice in 1981 (right).

Like the massive suffrage parade of March 3, 1913, the Women's March on Washington was planned around a presidential inauguration for January 21, 2017. More than 500,000 marchers gathered in a record-setting demonstration in Washington, DC (above) and more than 4,000,000 marched in cities around the world. Liza Donovan's poster for the march (right) features a liberty torch, a dove of peace, and hands representing many races, demanding *Hear Our Voice*.

Created nearly a century apart, these two magazine covers both feature an amended Declaration of Independence: on the left, Paul Stahr's July 1, 1915, cover for *Life*, and on the right, the cover for *TIME* from October 8, 2018.

BALLOT BOX

ENRIC

FURTHER READING

Note About Sources

This book is based on the research, scholarship, and writings of past and present Library of Congress staff, including Hannah Freece, Sheridan Harvey, Aimee Hess, Carroll Johnson, Cait Miller, Rosemary Fry Plakas, Janice E. Ruth, and Evelyn Sinclair.

In addition to a wealth of suffrage-related photographs, newspapers and periodicals, scrapbooks, music, and broadsides, the Library of Congress holds many specific collections pertinent to the study of woman suffrage. These include the records of the National American Woman Suffrage Association, the National Woman's Party, and the League of Women Voters; and the papers of many individuals important to the movement, including Susan B. Anthony, Elizabeth Cady Stanton, Frederick Douglass, the Blackwell Family, Mary Church Terrell, Carrie Chapman Catt, Harriot Stanton Blatch, and Nannie Helen Burroughs. Information about these collections can be found at www.loc.gov.

Further Reading

Allen, Jodie T. "Reluctant Suffragettes: When Women Questioned Their Right to Vote." Washington, DC: Pew Research Center, March 18, 2009.

Baker, Jean H., ed. *Votes for Women: The Struggle for Suffrage Revisited*. New York: Oxford University Press, 2002.

Walter J. Enright, *The Condescending Man*, published as the cover of *Harper's Weekly*, August 14, 1915 (detail).

Blackwell, Alice Stone. *Lucy Stone: Pioneer of Women's Rights*. Charlottesville: University Press of Virginia, 2001. First published 1930 by Little, Brown (Boston).

Bloomer, Dexter C. *The Life and Writings of Amelia Bloomer*. Boston: Arena Publishing Company, 1895.

Corder, J. Kevin and Wolbrecht, Christina. *Counting Women's Ballots: Female Voters from Suffrage through the New Deal*. New York: Cambridge University Press, 2016.

DuBois, Ellen Carol. *Woman Suffrage and Women's Rights*. New York: New York University Press, 1998.

Dudden, Faye E. *Fighting Chance: The Struggle over Woman Suffrage and Black Suffrage in Reconstruction America*. New York: Oxford University Press, 2011.

Florey, Kenneth. *Women's Suffrage Memorabilia: An Illustrated Historical Study*. McFarland & Company, 2013.

Franzen, Trisha. *Anna Howard Shaw: The Work of Woman Suffrage*. Urbana: University of Illinois Press, 2014.

Goodier, Susan. *No Votes for Women: The New York State Anti-Suffrage Movement*. Urbana: University of Illinois Press, 2013.

Gordon, Ann D., ed. *African American Women and the Vote, 1837–1965*. Amherst: University of Massachusetts Press, 1997.

———. *The Selected Papers of Elizabeth Cady Stanton and Susan B. Anthony*, 6 vols. New Brunswick, NJ: Rutgers University Press, 1997–2012.

Harrison, Patricia Greenwood. *Connecting Links: The British and American Woman Suffrage Movements, 1900–1914*. Westport, CT: Greenwood Press, 2000.

Keyssar, Alexander. *The Right to Vote: The Contested History of Democracy in the United States*. Revised edition. New York: Basic Books, 2000.

Kesselman, Amy. "'The "Freedom Suit': Feminism and Dress Reform in the United States, 1848–1875." *Gender and Society* 5, no. 4 (1991): 495–10.

Kroeger, Brooke. *The Suffragents: How Women Used Men to Get the Vote*. Albany: State University of New York Press, 2017.

Library of Congress. *American Women: A Library of Congress Guide for the Study of Women's History and Culture in the United States*. Washington, DC: US Government Printing Office, 2001.

Marshall, Susan E. *Splintered Sisterhood: Gender and Class in the Campaign Against Woman Suffrage*. Madison: University of Wisconsin Press, 1997.

Mead, Rebecca J. *How the Vote was Won: Woman Suffrage in the Western United States, 1868–1914*. New York: New York University Press, 2004.

Painter, Nell Irvin. *Sojourner Truth: A Life, A Symbol*. New York: W. W. Norton, 1996.

Ruth, Janice E. and Evelyn Sinclair. *Women Who Dare: Women of the Suffrage Movement*. San Francisco: Pomegranate Communications in association with the Library of Congress, 2006.

Stanton, Elizabeth Cady, Susan B. Anthony, Matilda Joslyn Gage et al. *History of Woman Suffrage*, 6 vols. (vols. 1–2, New York: Fowler & Wells, 1881, 1882; vol. 3, Rochester, NY: Susan B. Anthony, 1886; vol. 4, Rochester, NY: Susan B. Anthony, 1902; vols. 5–6, New York: National American Woman Suffrage Association, 1922).

Stevens, Doris. *Jailed for Freedom*. New York: Boni and Liveright, 1920.

Stovall, James Glen. *Seeing Suffrage: The Washington Suffrage Parade of 1913, Its Pictures, and Its Effect on the American Political Landscape*. Knoxville: University of Tennessee Press, 2013.

Tetrault, Lisa. *The Myth of Seneca Falls: Memory and the Women's Suffrage Movement, 1848–1898*. Chapel Hill: University of North Carolina Press, 2014.

Terborg-Penn, Rosalyn. *African American Women in the Struggle for the Vote, 1850–1920*. Bloomington: Indiana University Press, 1998.

Thurner, Manuela. "'Better Citizens Without the Ballot': American AntiSuffrage Women and Their Rationale During the Progressive Era." *Journal of Women's History* 5, no. 1 (1993): 33–60.

Tickner, Lisa. *The Spectacle of Women: Imagery of the Suffrage Campaign, 1907–14*. Chicago: University of Chicago Press, 1988.

Van Voris, Jacqueline. *Carrie Chapman Catt: A Public Life*. New York: The Feminist Press at the City University of New York, 1987.

Wheeler, Marjorie Spruill. *New Women of the New South: The Leaders of the Woman Suffrage Movement in the Southern States*. New York: Oxford University Press, 1993.

Zahniser, J. D., and Amelia Fry. *Alice Paul: Claiming Power*. New York: Oxford University Press, 2014.

INDEX

ILLUSTRATION CREDITS

All images are from the collections of the Library of Congress unless otherwise noted. Images from the Library's Prints and Photographs Division can be viewed or downloaded at loc.gov/pictures. Many items from other divisions can be viewed or downloaded from the Library's online catalog at catalog.loc.gov. For assistance, contact the appropriate custodial division or Duplication Services (loc.gov/duplicationservices).

The following abbreviations appear throughout the image credits:

AMED: African and Middle Eastern Division
GC: General Collections
G&M: Geography and Maps Division
LAW: Law Library of Congress
MSS: Manuscript Division
MUS: Music Division
NAWSA: National American Woman Suffrage Association
NWP: National Woman's Party
P&P: Prints and Photographs Division
RBSC: Rare Books and Special Collections Division
SER: Serial and Government Periodicals Division

Front Matter

The title and logo font is 19th by Pure+Applied, custom designed for "Shall Not Be Denied."
Cover: MSS, NWP Records, II:276
Opposite title page: P&P, LC-DIG-hec-10354; also in MSS, NWP Records, I:160
Opposite Table of Contents: P&P, LC-DIG-hec-03677
vi: P&P, LC-DIG-ds-12370
viii: P&P, LC-USZ62-135533
ix: P&P, LC-USZC2-1199
x: P&P, LC-DIG-ppmsca-25513

Chapter 1

2: G&M, LCCN 96684621
3 (left): MSS, NAWSA Records, Container 76
3 (right): RBSC, HQ1596 .W6 1792a (Anthony Coll)
4 (left): Collection of the Massachusetts Historical Society
4 (right): LAW, LCCN 07019321
5: RBSC, E185 .A254 container C, no. 50
6: MSS, NWP Records, Group II, Container II:275
7: RBSC, JK1881 .N357 sec. 1, No. 162
8: P&P, LC-USZ62-48965
9: MSS, Elizabeth Cady Stanton Papers, Container 9
10: P&P, LC-DIG-ds-07422
11: P&P, LC-DIG-ds-13015

Suffragist holding banner, 1917 (detail).

12: MSS, Carrie Chapman Catt Papers, Box 30

13 (left): P&P, LC-DIG-ds-13019

13 (right): P&P, LC-DIG-ds-13012

14 (left): P&P, LC-USZ6-2055

14 (right): P&P, LC-USZ62-76998

15 (left): MSS, Blackwell Family Papers, Box 81

15 (right): MSS, Blackwell Family, Lucy Stone, Box 85, Folder: Speech Announcements

17: P&P, LC-DIG-pga-01767

18: P&P, LC-DIG-ppmsca-08978

19 (left): MSS, NWP Records, II:276

19 (right): P&P, LC-USZ62-118946

20: P&P, LC-USZ62-33275

21 (left): P&P, LC-DIG-ppmsca-58145

21 (right): P&P, LC-DIG-ds-13016

22: RBSC, Susan B. Anthony Collection, JK1899. A6 A5

23 (left): MSS, Susan B. Anthony Papers, Box 4

23 (right): GC, AP4.I3

24: P&P, LC-DIG-pga-05762

25: P&P, LC-DIG-ppmsca-50302

26 (right): P&P, LC-DIG-ppmsca-50312

27 (left): P&P, LC-USZ62-54722

27 (right): RBSC, E449 .D16 vol. A, no. 13

29 (left): P&P, LC-DIG-ggbain-05640

29 (right): RBSC, HV6201 .N2

29 (bottom): GC, PZ3.A79

30 (left): MSS, NWP Records, II:275

30 (right): P&P, LC-DIG-ppmsca-25513

31: P&P, LC-USZ61-787

32: P&P, LC-DIG-ds-13020

33: P&P, LC-USZC4-4119

Chapter 2

34: P&P, LC-DIG-ppmsca-04664

36: RBSC, Miller NAWSA Suffrage Scrapbook 6

37 (left): MSS, NAWSA Records, Box 72

37 (right): P&P, LC-DIG-ggbain-09988

38: P&P, LC-DIG-ds-12367

39: P&P, LC-DIG-stereo-1s16054

40 (left): P&P, LC-DIG-ppmsca-34349

40 (right): GC, AP101 .L6

41 (left): P&P, LC-DIG-ppmsca-55836

41 (right): GC, AP101 .L6

42, 43, and 44 (left): RBSC, Miller NAWSA Suffrage Scrapbook 9

44 (right): P&P, LC-DIG-ggbain-14077

45: P&P, LC-DIG-ds-13021

46: MSS, NAWSA Records, Box 95

47 (left): MSS, NAWSA, Box 76. Also in NWP Records, I:2

47 (right): GC, AP101 .L6

48: MSS, NAWSA Records, Box 95

49: GC, JK1880 .W58

51 (left): P&P, LC-USZ62-25338

51 (right): P&P, LC-DIG-ppmsca-27952

52 (left): MSS, NAWSA Records, Box 76

52 (right): GC, AP2 .H32

53: MSS, NAWSA Records, Box 97

54: P&P, LC-DIG-ds-12369

55 (left): P&P, LC-DIG-hec-05374

55 (right): MSS, NAWSA Records, LC-MSS-34132-7

56: MUS, M1665.W8 H

57 (left): AMED, Hebraic Section, Yiddish Sheet Music, Box 4 – 416

57 (right): MUS, M1665.W8 H

58: MUS, M1665.W8 P

59 (left): MUS, M1665.W8 E

59 (right): MUS, M1665.W8 H

60: P&P, LC-DIG-ggbain-11476

61 (left): P&P, LC-DIG-ppmsca-12512

61 (right): P&P, LC-DIG-ppmsc-00031

62 (left): P&P, LC-USZ62-107756

62 (right): P&P, LC-USZ62-70382

63: GC, HQ1101 .W6

Chapter 3

64: MSS, NWP Records, II:276

66: P&P, LC-DIG-ggbain-13707

67: MSS, NWP Records, I:160

68: MSS, NWP Records, I:160

69: GC, TX715 .K63

70 (left and right): MSS, Breckinridge Family Papers, Container 705

71 (left): MSS, NAWSA Records, Box 72

71 (right): MSS, Breckinridge Family Papers, Container 703

72 (left): MSS, League of Women Voters Records, III:143

72 (right): MSS, Harriot Stanton Blatch Papers, Box 11

73: MSS, NAWSA Records, Box 97

74: P&P, LC-USZ62-106646

75: P&P, LC-DIG-hec-04154

76: MSS, NAWSA Records, Box 11

77 (left): P&P, LC-USZC4-5585

77 (right): P&P, LC-DIG-ggbain-18952

78: MSS, NWP Records, I:160

79: P&P, LC-DIG-hec-07525

80 (left): P&P, LC-DIG-hec-07113

80 (right): MSS, NWP Records, I:159

81: MSS, NWP Records, II:274

82 (top): P&P, LC-DIG-hec-09043

82 (bottom): P&P, LC-DIG-hec-09041

83 (top): MSS, NWP Records, I:160

83 (bottom): MSS, NWP Records, II:276

84 (left): MSS, NWP Records, I:160

84 (right): MSS, NWP Records, I:81

85: MSS, NWP Records, II:276

86: MSS, NWP Records, I:160

87 (left): MSS, NAWSA Records, Box 95

87 (right): P&P, LC-DIG-ds-13018

88: GC, JK1880 .W58

89: MSS, Harriot Stanton Blatch Papers, Box 7

90: P&P, LC-USZ62-110995

91 (left): MSS, NAWSA Records, Box 91

91 (right): MSS, NWP Records, II:276

92: SER, LCCN sn83030214

93 (left): P&P, LC-USZ62-75334

93 (right): P&P, LC-USZC2-6247

94 (left): P&P, LC-DIG-ppmsca-56874

94 (right): MSS, NWP Records, II:276

96 (left): MSS, NWP Records, II:276

96 (right): P&P, LC-DIG-ppmsca-37807

97 (left): MSS, NWP Records, I:160

97 (right): MSS, Carrie Chapman Catt Papers, Box 30

98: MSS, NWP Records, Box IV: 7

99: GC, JK1880 .W58

Chapter 4

100: P&P, LC-DIG-ds-13017. Courtesy of
Liza Donovan

102: P&P, LC-DIG-npcc-12394

103 (left): MSS, NWP Records, I:160

103 (right): MSS, League of Women Voters Records,
Part I, Box 87, OV

105 (left): SER, LCCN sn83025353

105 (right): P&P, LC-DIG-ds-13013

106 (left): P&P, LC-DIG-ds-13014

106 (right): P&P, LC-DIG-ppmsca-03066. A 1965
Herblock cartoon, copyright The Herb Block
Foundation

107: MSS, NWP Records, II:200

108: P&P, LC-DIG-ds-04461. © Bettye Lane Photos

109 (left): P&P, LC-DIG-ppmsca-42048

109 (right): P&P, LC-DIG-ppmsca-31216. Marilyn
Church Artist

110 (top): Benjamin Lowy/Getty Images News/Getty
Images

110 (bottom): P&P, LC-DIG-ds-13017. Courtesy of
Liza Donovan

111 (left): GC, AP101 .L6

111 (right): From TIME, October 8, 2018 © 2018
Time Inc. Used under license. TIME and Time Inc.
are not affiliated with, and do not endorse products or services of Licensee.

Back Matter

112: GC, AP2 .H32

124: P&P, LC-DIG-hec-09850